MW01034142

MISUNDERSTANDING
BOKO HARAM

Understanding the historic and ethnic causes of
Nigeria's fundamentalist terrorist group

DR. DARLINGTON AKAISO

Copyright © 2018 by Dr. Darlington Akaiso

All rights reserved. No part of this work covered by the
copyrights hereon may be reproduced or used in any form or by any
means – graphic, electronic or mechanical, including
photocopying, recording, taping or
information storage and retrieval systems –
without the prior written permission of the publisher.

Library and Archives Canada Cataloguing in Publication

CIP data on file with the National Library and Archives

ISBN trade paperback 978-1-55483-867-7
ISBN e-book 978-1-55483-868-4

Disclaimer:

The views expressed in this publication are those of the author and do
not necessarily represent those of any of the global international
development agencies, organizations or higher education institutions,
the publisher may have served, or currently works for.

The author has made every effort to ensure the accuracy of the
information within this book was correct at time of publication. Any
world wide web (www) address or hypertext link (http:) referenced in
this publication was considered functional at press time. Considering
the constantly changing and dynamic nature of the internet, some of the
information associated with these web and hypertext link (http:)
addresses may have been modified, changed or removed after the
publication. Acknowledging the possibility of this inconvenience, the
author does not assume and hereby disclaims any liability to any party
for any damage, caused by errors or omissions, whether such errors or
omissions result from accident, negligence, or any other cause.

Foreword

It is an honor to write this foreword for Dr. Darlington Akaiso's new book, *Misunderstanding Boko Haram*. I have known Dr. Akaiso since he began his doctoral work in Franklin Pierce University Doctor of Leadership Program about a decade ago. As a faculty member and advisor, my work is to encourage a new generation of intellectuals to find their path. For Dr. Akaiso, his passion was understanding the complexities of non-western regions of the world. At the time, he worked in International Risk Management and developing appropriate response techniques to international crises. Even then, he was adamant that responses by international aid should be appropriate for individuals and families in the particular regions (often rural) and not just a prefabricated response designed for all, it is an exciting puzzle that he brooches in this manuscript. This particular writing details just how critical his work is. What Dr. Akaiso has been and still is an understanding that many countries (often developed during and after World War I) are social constructions of place, developed by post-colonial countries such as Great Britain. In this book he examines Nigeria where he was born and raised. He still has family there and visits as frequently as possible. By viewing many places, such as Nigeria, as a country fabricated from the western concept of a national politic, Dr. Akaiso warns us that we lack an understanding of many international events.

In this book, Dr. Akaiso defies our understanding by directly tackling the role of Boko Haram as a particular event that directly involves the international community. What better example to offer in his attempt at deconstructing the nature of this particular crisis within the realm of international affairs. By examining the genesis of Nigeria and the history of the regions therein and by focusing on geography and ethnicity as well, he is carefully unraveling western conceptions of cause and effect. Throughout this book, Dr. Akaiso carefully unravels the tapestry of our assumptions and weaves a narrative that is not based on individualism but on interdependence. As we examine the origin of British colonized Nigeria, the reality of tribal conflict, and the emerging concept of "enthnoregionalism," our understanding of events shifts. When one recognizes the interrelationship of human welfare, where an individual's welfare depends not only on their behaviors, needs, and survival but on those of others—we are forced to recognize that individual choices are dependent upon others' choices and others' actions. The western world which prides itself on individualism has difficulty grasping the concept of interrelatedness. Perhaps if we can understand that we are all struggling for the same thing—a legacy for our children and families and community—we can develop a framework based on understanding rather than blame and accusation and immediate, decisive action. Although this book is aimed at a Nigerian response to Boko Haram, it also includes the greater sub-Saharan African and the international communities. Dr. Akaiso articulates this so masterfully when he brings us closer to a particular ethnic group (Boko Haraam) to understand their being. And it is a wonderful reminder for me of Dr. Akaiso's legacy as a doctoral student, helping his colleagues to interpret events, not through a veil of personal biases and assumptions. Rather, he encourages us to reach for something at once far more complicated yet so simple. Crises do not arise in a vacuum.

Maggie Moore-West Ph.D., MA, MSW
Professor, Franklin Pierce University, NH. USA (2004-2015)
Instructor, Geisel School of Medicine at Dartmouth, College. USA

This book joins a host of other works on the development of Boko Haram in Nigeria and provides a unique perspective. Dr. Akaiso has done important and extensive research on the geographic, historic, and governance factors that have influenced the emergence and evolution of Boko Haram. It contributes to the literature by providing a clearer picture of the underlying elements that impact this group's development and sustenance and explores options for resolving issues that enable its continuation.

Dr. Grace Klinefelter
Formerly Dean, School of Business,
Virginia International University. Fairfax, VA. USA

Food for Thought

Take a moment to ponder over the following. Maybe these realities may turn on some light bulbs.

This book does not have a religious connotation or undertone as readers may have expected. However, it looks at Boko Haram from a deeper perspective which is its foundational ethnicity. *The arguments* on why this book is not veering the religious course are numerous, with the most outstanding being, if the cause of the Boko Haram insurgency was purely religious, then how come its base isn't in north-central or northwestern Nigeria where we have the kano or Sokoto religious strongholds.

- *Why* is the Boko Haram insurgency rooted in northeast nigeria?
- *Why* should this self-acclaimed religious movement defy the dominant religious stronghold of the north central or northwestern nigeria?
- *Why* should Boko Haram insurgency take up the course of fighting this religious war on behalf of the greater northern Hausa Fulani dominated north?

Think about this again. Some context here may help. The above statements are analogous to a man from Ondo state in Nigeria, fighting for the stool and root of the Yorubas against the Oyo Empire or the Kogi indigenes fighting the ancestral dynasty of the Bini kingdom against the Binis.

These and a few other leads have left the author no other choice but to silently investigate other factors as the bearing on which the Boko Haram movement has been founded on. A further examination of the contents of this book will go along to present astonishing facts other authors may have strayed away from.

Preface

Although a plethora of theories have been advanced and various perspectives taken to explain the phenomenon of Boko Haram insurgency in the northeastern part of Nigeria, very little has been done to understudy the cause of how Boko Haram came into being or even the fundamental dynamics of the elements that have sustained this insurgency. Given the common knowledge that majority of the insurgents are Kanuri ethnics in the northeast of Nigeria, it becomes imperative to reassess the past and present relations between the Kanuri people and the huge Hausa/Fulani population dominating the northern part of the country.

This work would not fail to recognize the age-long Kanuri resentment of the Hausa/Fulani hegemony in the region, and at the same time, it would bring to the fore the historical rivalry that originated out of stiff resistance of Fulani jihadists by Kanuri's old Borno Empire in the nineteenth century. As it is rightly noted, the old Borno Empire that covered the area of the present-day Borno and Yobe States, including parts of Niger, Chad, and Cameroon, was not conquered by the Fulani jihadists. Hence contempt amongst the ethnic nationalities persists to this day. The result of the contempt has been the marginalization of the Kanuri in the northeastern region by the Hausa/Fulani majority.

Secondarily, the semi-unconscious role played by the Nigerian government itself where ethnic-based apparatuses were not only employed but drawn upon at various times may have automatically advanced a damaging sectional agenda in the country. By deploying geopolitical, traditional, and ethnic movements in its bid to stem the tides of unrest and resolve regional and sectarian crisis in the country, the Nigerian government indisputably empowered various movements across the country. These movements include the southeast's Movement for the Actualization of the of Sovereign State of Biafra (MASSOB), southwest's Oodua People's Congress (OPC), south-south's Movement for the Emancipation of Niger Delta (MEND), and north's Arewa People's Congress (APC). The writer would like you to pay careful attention to the following permutation used to adjudicate geopolitical and tribal issues throughout the country.

Sovereign State of Biafra (MASSOB), southwest's Oodua People's Congress (OPC), south's Movement for the Emancipation of Niger Delta (MEND), and north's Arewa People's Congress (APC). The writer would like you to pay careful attention to the following permutation used to adjudicate geopolitical and tribal issues throughout the country.

- MASSOB chieftains (chiefs, ruler, elders, or even warlords in some cases)—southeast
- OPC chieftains (chiefs, ruler, elders, or even warlords in some cases)—southwest
- MEND chieftains (chiefs, ruler, elders, or even warlords in some cases)—south-south
- APC chieftains (chiefs, ruler, elders, or even warlords in some cases)—northwest and central
- Afenifere chieftains (chiefs, ruler, elders, or even warlords

in some cases)—southwest

- Ndigbo chieftains (chiefs, ruler, elders, or even warlords in some cases)—southeast and central

Without requiring any mathematical formula, one can see that the northeast has been left out of this equation. Knowing full well of how, unfortunately, financial settlements play a key role in Nigeria's democracy. One is left with no other choice but to agree with that fact that there is no provision to service the chieftains of the Kanuri northeast. Tell me, how then will they play their legislative role in advocating for peace in their region? Even if they try, the domineering Arewa People's Congress will allow them no place on the resolution council table. Given this backdrop, this study is of clear arguments that it is the marginalization of the Kanuri that deepens frustration in the northeastern region and that Boko Haram insurgency, despite its claimed Islamic objectives, is the mask of Kanuri's revolt against the rest of the north and the Nigerian state.

In attempting to confirm Boko Haram as a northeast ethnic militia, the author would draw from the experience of unrest in the country. This would be done by discussing the activities of the southeast's Movement for the Actualization of the Sovereign State of Biafra (MASSOB), southwest's Oodua People's Congress (OPC), south's Movement for the Emancipation of Niger Delta (MEND), Afenifere, Ohaneze Ndigbo, Arewa, and north's Arewa People's Congress (APC) describing them as ethnic-based apparatuses employed at various times to advance sectional agenda in the country. This book would also show that effective ethnic sociocultural arrangements, such as MASSOB, OPC, MEND, APC, Afenifere, Ohaneze Ndigbo, and Arewa, had been very useful from time to time in stemming the tides of unrest in the country.

Analogical to the spilled milk scenario, the human and societal damage caused by the Boko Haram insurgency has been way forgone. However, an attempt to raise a formidable Kanuri sociocultural structure, giving it a strong voice and power, no doubt would contribute in no small measures in bringing peace back to the battered northeastern part of the country.

CHAPTER 1

Introduction

The Missing Voice of Kanuri in Boko Haram Insurgency

Boko Haram insurgents, in the most basic sense, are humans. They have families; they grow amongst their relatives and appreciate both the pleasure and value of associating with their kindred. They are not without affection for their families, communities, and fellow ethnics, especially in the face of competing interests with outsiders. On the other hand, they do not lack those that would sympathize with them and pray they survive in the course of their terror campaigns. Each time a Boko Haram terrorist is killed on a mission, it is probable that the killing would embitter their loved ones and enrage them to the point of seeking revenge through the same terror mechanism. The tendency to avenge the death of their own has helped a great deal in swelling the terrorists' camps in a very rapid manner. Indeed, the vengeful recruits are easily accommodated and probably adjust to life in the militias' camp in a more convenient and effective manner since the handlers of the whole structure of terrorism are of their stock and could speak to them in their mother's tongue which goes straight to their hearts as Nelson Mandela would say.

Boko Haram sects may base their foundation on religious

reasons, but such reasons alone could not have sufficed to sustain their terror campaign if not for the ethnic retaliatory tendency and the quest for self-preservation amongst other secondary factors this book will unveil. The book does not have a strong religious connotation or undertone as the reader may have expected. It looks at Boko Haram from a deeper perspective which centers on ethnicity. If the insurgency was a purely religious revolution, then perhaps the epicenter would have expanded to, if not overtaken by a more active religious war theatre of northwestern or north-central geopolitical zones of Nigeria. The factors brought forth to explain why this work is not following the religious course may be numerous, but the most outstanding question interrogates the reason Boko Haram movement deviated from securing a permanent home in the dominant religious crisis flashpoints of the northwest or north central Nigeria but prefer northeast.

Yes! The author links Boko Haram insurgency to ethnicity. But which particular ethnic group is he referring to? The gross misunderstanding involved in understudying the phenomenon of Boko Haram extremist Islamism stems from a lot of outsiders who tend to refer to all northern Nigerians as Hausa/Fulani without taking cognizance of the distinct ethnic minorities such as Kanuri, Jukun, Tiv, Nupe, Adamawa, Gwuari, and several others living in the northern half of Nigeria. Looking at the ethnic composition of Boko Haram militants, both leadership and the sect's ranks and files are dominated by Kanuri ethnic group. This group largely occupy the northeast of Nigeria, especially Borno, Adamawa, Yobe, Bauchi, and Gombe States. Neighboring countries of Chad,

Niger, and the Cameroons also house various sizes of Kanuri populations which accounts for the presence of their nationals in the militant ranks and files. In all the concepts advanced to explain the phenomenon of Boko Haram insurrections, one good argument that surprisingly escapes the emphasis of many writers is the notion that Boko Haram is serving as an ethnic mechanism expressing Kanuri grievances against the hegemony of Hausa/Fulani ethnics in the north and by extension, the Nigerian state.

Another reason that captured the writer's attention has to do with the duration of the insurgency. If Boko Haram was purely a religious war, then religious forces alone would not have sustained it that long. Nigeria has witnessed fair counts of religious-based crises since independence. These crises mostly occur in a spasmodic manner. None endured so long as Boko Haram. At the location it was incubated, the character of Boko Haram was circumstantially and dramatically transformed from Islamic movement to an ethnic apparatus by the milieus of ethnic Kanuri of northeastern Nigeria. A careful look at Maitatsine, which claimed about five thousand lives in the northwest of Nigeria in the early 1980s and considered the forerunner of the religious terrorism in Nigeria, unlike Boko Haram, they lacked ethnic basis. Maitatsine's lack of ethnic character could be explained based on the fact that its founder, Alhaji Mohammed Marwa, was not a Nigerian. He migrated from the town of Maroua in northern Cameroon to Kano in 1945. But his strange teachings thrilled and attracted followership from the jobless and the downtrodden populations living in the slums of Kano. Instead of one ethnic group dominating the membership of Maitatsine, it became a movement for the urban poor.

One apt discovery is that Boko Haram came to win greater support than its forerunner, Maitatsine. This and a few other leads have left the author with no other choice but to steadfastly dig deeper. Maitatsine was an Islamic sect with strong anti-Western sentiments, posturing the same way like Boko Haram before it was overtaken by parochial ethnic agenda. Both sects embraced Islamic radicalism. Maitatsine militancy was sparked off by the murder of Marwa's son Tijani by the security operatives the way Boko Haram was amplified by the killing of the sect's mourners and the summary execution of its leader, Mohammed Yusuf. Unlike Boko Haram that won the support of powerful Kanuri elements, Maitatsine was condemned by the privileged class and the mainstream Muslims in the north because Marwa teachings were found as contradicting the Islamic norms. For example, Marwa would claim Prophet Muhammad was not the messenger of Allah; he would reject the hadith and the sunna and regarded the reading of any other books apart from the Koran as an act of paganism. Mohammed Marwa would speak against the use of Western innovations, like television, radio, watches, bicycle, cars, and condemned excessive use of more money. While Boko Haram militants were equipped with sophisticated firearms, explosives, and vehicles, Maitatsine insurgents were using crude weapons such as clubs, Dane guns, stones, bow, and arrows. Because of its weak support base, Maitatsine was easily routed by the forces of the Nigerian government. But with Boko Haram, it is a different ball game.

Of course, there is a long history of tension between

Hausa/Fulani and Kanuri which could be traced to the early nineteenth century. In 1809, after important Hausa states of Zaria, Katsina, and Kano had all came under the control of the Fulani jihadists led by Uthman dan Fodio and his son Mohammed Bello, the Fulani with Hausa elements was to turn their attention to Kanuri's domain, Bornu, where they recorded some success until the Mai of Bornu appealed to Muhammed Al-Kanemi who succeeded in repulsing the jihadists and establishing Shehu dynasty that would come to rival Fulani's Sokoto Caliphate in the northwest. Therefore, the existing history that old Bornu or Kanuri Empire was not brought under the control of the jihadists remains a matter of envy for succeeding generations of Hausa/Fulani Muslims and a thing of pride for Kanuri ethnic nationalities living in the northeast of Nigeria. With this historical grudge existing side by side with Hausa/Fulani's tendency to dominate the entire north, the Kanuri could not help being jumped at any cause that would save their identity from being eclipsed by Hausa/Fulani hegemony.

It is worthy of note that Kanuri people in the northeast are not taking religious and traditional directives from Fulani-controlled Sokoto Caliphate in the northwest but from Shehu of Kanuri Bornu. This could be significant in creating doctrinal tussling that aide the formation and the growth of Boko Haram in Nigeria.

However, ethnic rivalry is a common problem that holds sway in Nigeria. As a multiethnic nation, Nigeria is deeply divided along ethnic lines. Besides religious differences, ethnic conflicts constitute the basis of the country's many crises. In Nigeria, groups are perennially bent on competing and prevailing over the interests of other ethnic nationalities. This situation contributes immensely to several outbreaks of violent conflicts in the country. Consequently, several ethnic militias have sprouted in the face of a pugnacious drive to advance ethnoregional agenda—this often led to wanton destruction of human lives, public infrastructures, and private properties.

Almost all parts of Nigeria have witnessed ethnoregional insurrections steered by ethnic militias. For example, O'odua People's Congress (OPC) was established in the Yoruba-speaking southwest in 1994 to demonstrate their grievance towards the annulment of 1993 elections in which Chief M. K. O. Abiola, a Yoruba man, seemingly won the presidency. In the southeast region, the Movement for the Actualization of the Sovereign State of Biafra (MASSOB) representing Igbo ethnic group was set in place to give teeth to the Igbo cause as they sought the independent state of Biafra, owing to the perception that Igbo people have grossly and systematically been marginalized after the civil war in 1970. In the oil-bearing south-south region, Movement for the Emancipation of the Niger Delta (MEND) emerged from 2006, serving as a blanket militia organization for several rebel groups in the area. MEND coordinated a series of attacks on oil installations, took foreign oil workers hostage in order to cripple oil production, and fought government forces to help draw the world's attention to the poverty, unemployment, wanton ecological damage, and unjust revenue allocation in Niger Delta region. This region generates most of the nation's foreign revenue.

The northern part of the country has not been without its

breed of militant group. The Arewa People's Congress (APC) interestingly represents the ambition of the core north. The group came into existence in 1999. Unlike other ethnic militias that sought alteration of the status quo, the Arewa People's Congress was aiming at maintaining the state of affairs to the benefits of the northerners.

The semi-unconscious role played by the Nigerian government itself where these ethnoregional apparatuses were not only employed but drawn upon at various times may have automatically advanced a damaging sectional agenda in the country. By deploying geopolitical, traditional, and ethnic movements in its bid to stem the tides of unrest and resolve regional and sectarian crisis in the country, the Nigerian government indisputably empowered various movements across the country.

Although Boko Haram movement is claimed to have been founded on pure Islamic grounds, circumstances have helped it flourish on ethnic factor. Some evidence suggests that the initial approach adopted by the organization was relatively nonviolent. Ustaz Muhammed Yusuf, a Kanuri to whom the founding of the sect is now generally ascribed, was quoted by Agence France-Presse in January 2006 as saying that an Islamic system of government should be established in Nigeria and if possible, all over the world but through dialogue. He was said to be against all forms of violence, saying they contradict the teachings of Islam. But the brutal response of the security forces to the activities of Boko Haram prompted Yusuf to declare war on the people of Nigeria, putting down in the leaflet titled Maye Ya Manta, meaning if the perpetrators have forgotten, the victims will not. This could help in explaining why the character of the Islamists dramatically changed position from nonviolence posturing to the nature of bellicosity owing to retaliatory drive.

Attacks by Nigerian security forces on Boko Haram suspects had wrought heavy casualty on the Kanuri ethnic nationalities. The summary execution of Yusuf by the police in 2009 fueled the Kanuri antagonism towards Nigerian state more than ever. Consequently, the sect's violent operations were to increase in frequency and intensity after Abubakar Shekau, another Kanuri, took over the control of the Islamic sect. The increase in non-Kanuri targets suggested that behind the religious mask of Boko Haram Islamic sects, there was an ethnic agenda.

Unlike other ethnoregional militias that emerged with clear-cut aims and objectives, Boko Haram was gradually undergoing changes to accommodate political, socioeconomic, and religious yearnings of its host Kanuri ethnic group. The glorious history, the Islamic heritage, and gross marginalization altogether offered a fertile ground in the northeast for the seed of Islamic radicalism to grow into a gigantic umbrella tree that covers all forms of sectional interests. Boko Haram would become a big stick wielded by Kanuri overlords to bludgeon Nigeria into succumbing to their ethnic agenda. Therefore what OPC, MASSOB, MEND, APC, and MEND meant to their respective regions now becomes the same thing Boko Haram means for the Kanuri.

CHAPTER 2
Ethnic Origins and Concepts of Nigerian Crises
A Background to Boko Haram Insurgency

There was no nation under the sun named Nigeria until British imperialists brought with them the wind of colonialism beginning from the last quarter of the nineteenth century. All that existed prior to the colonial era within the geographical confines of what is now called Nigeria were independent empires, kingdoms, vassal states, and several other splinter groups. As distinct nations in their own right, these groups had fashioned their traditional way of governance long before the arrival of the colonial masters. As the vast area came to be christened *Nigeria* by a British woman Ms. Flora Shaw in 1897 followed by the amalgamation of 1914, northern and southern protectorates of Nigeria, both harboring more than three hundred nations were lumped together to form a single government. The stage was set and opened for these diverse nations to struggle for space, resources, identities, and their very existence under an alien, strange rule. As Leo Otoide puts, "Each group adopted strategies to survive and make the best of the problematic union."[1] He was to describe the amalgamation as a colonial fiat attempting to weld into one quite disparate collectivity, groups whose autonomy had been preserved for centuries.[2] Like other colonial act, Otoide stressed that it was primarily intended to serve the economic and political interest of the colonialists. The view of the victims of partition, those who bore the brunt of amalgamation was irrelevant and in any case not considered.[3]

Amalgamation was the assemblage of the strange bedfellows whose aspirations were conditioned by their differing historical experiences and cultural heritage. In his book *Path to Nigerian Freedom,* Chief Obafemi Awolowo aptly dismissed the notion of Nigeria's status as a nation. According to him, "It is a mere geographical expression. There are no 'Nigerian' in the same sense as there are 'English,' 'Welsh,' or 'French.' The word 'Nigeria' is merely a distinctive appellation to distinguish those who live within the boundaries of Nigeria from those who do not."[4]

Since Nigeria is a conglomeration of differing groups, there must be a collective commitment of each group to act in their self-interest without recourse to others' expectations. Of course, groups possess the attributes of humans. They crave prestige, power, wealth, identity and seek self-preservation. This is what Felix Airoboman of the department of philosophy in the University of Benin, Nigeria, called *social egoism.* With social egoism, there arose a tendency for tribalism. Airoboman wrote the following:

> Tribalism is a form of social egoism. It undermines the interest of other ethnic groups and insensates their needs and aspirations in favor of self-tribe. It agitates for the interests of one's group or its member(s) in the distribution of resources, positions, and privileges, whether they are (best) qualified for them or not. It also involves unjust criticism of other ethnic groups

or their members. As a form of social egoism, tribalism involves unjust defense or undue protection of those in one's ethnic group when they err. It also undermines the collective will or the common interest of a nation as a homogenous entity in favor of homogeneous common interest.[5]

Since the amalgamation of 1914 came out of arbitrariness on the part of British colonial masters without considering the expectations of the composite elements, the unity was to be sustained in crises. Loyalties to ethnic groups undermined the stability and the very existence of Nigeria as a state. According to Ehimika Ifidon, "The notions of equality and justice lose their ordinary meaning in multi-national states."[6] Ethnicity serves as a basis for exclusion.[7] Almost all sections making up Nigeria tend to pursue their interests without minding the dangers posed on the unity and the very life of the country.

In tracing the time ethnicity started to exert a profound influence on the life of the country, Robert Melson and Howard Wolpe maintained that the origin of ethnicity in Nigeria could not be dated earlier than the last decades of the colonial period when the new form of linguistic and cultural identities emerged. They noted that the period was characterized by the fusion and communal boundaries.[8] This would be the time the idea of a Yoruba race, an Igbo nation, and Hausa/Fulani identity would take root.[9] This development was signaled by the formation of sociocultural organizations in the colonial urban centers. Central to this formation was the improvement of the welfare of their members and by extension, the safeguarding of their ethnic interests. According to R. T. Akinyele, these organizations "emulated one another particularly in the award of scholarships and building of community schools."[10] It should be noted here that Ibibio State Union which drew membership from the present-day Akwa Ibom State was the foremost sociocultural group established in 1927. This organization established the Ibibio State College in Ikot Ekpene awarded scholarships to its members and helped in great measures in quelling the Aba Women's Riot of 1929. The activities of Ibibio State Union in the all-round development of the country won the organization the admiration and support of the colonial masters. Other ethnic groups were to take a cue from this developmental model and in due course came with their groupings.

Sociocultural unionism was not without its dangers. On this note, Ayodeji Olukoju pointed out that the politicization of the cultural union marked the beginning of ethnic politics in Nigeria.[11] There are two notable political figures that would not go without blames—Dr. Nnamdi Azikiwe, an Igbo man, and Chief Obafemi Awolowo, a Yoruba man. As Akinyele asserted, "Azikiwe is known to have committed a political blunder by affirming the right of the Igbos to lead the other ethnic groups in Africa in his acceptance speech as President of Igbo State Union."[12] J. S. Coleman and other authors noted that this claim injected poison into the cordial relationship that had existed among the cultural groups and forced many of them, like Edo, Ijaw, and others to form their ethnic unions for self-protection.[13] The formation by Yoruba's Egbe Omo Oduduwa in 1948 by Awolowo was to be viewed by Igbo ethnics as a declaration of war.

The evidence further suggested that Dr. Nnamdi Azikiwe was the one that infused ethnic sentiments into The Nigerian Youth Movement (NYM)—one of the earliest political parties in Nigeria which came into existence in 1934. Azikiwe was quoted to have made ethnically-oriented comments when Ernest Ikoli, who was supported by the likes of Chief Obafemi Awolowo and H. O. Davies, won 1941 presidential election of the movement against his preferred candidate, Samuel Akisanya. Dr. Nnamdi Azikiwe was to rationalize the defeat by saying that his candidate lost the election because he (Azikiwe) was not a Yoruba man.[14] Consequently, Azikiwe and loyal Igbo elements resigned their membership from the movement. Ever since, according to Haruna Dlakwa, "The paranoia, rather than concrete proof of victimization on ethnic grounds has become the driving force of ethnic relations in the country."[15]

The activities of Chief Obafemi Awolowo had also been found as contributing in exacerbating the vice of ethnicity in the country during the last decades of the colonial period. The formation of the political party Action Group (AG) by Yoruba intellectuals and businessmen with Awolowo as the leader was to be embroiled in ethnic coloration. Mokwugo Okoye documented that AG started in March 1950 as an arm of action committee of the Egbe Omo Oduduwa and was thus suckled in tribalism from the start. According to him, it was led by a handful of ambitious masterminds bent on salvaging their class and tribal interests from an amalgam of a composite Nigerian nation; its leitmotif was "Western (Nigerian) Solidarity," and it showed at once that it did not care much for the rest of the country.[16]

After Nigeria attained sovereign statehood in 1960, the ground was further cleared for ethnic competition among Igbos, Yorubas, and Hausas/Fulanis, with minorities struggling for prominence. In observing the nature of ethnicity in the politics of the first republic, Chief Awolowo admitted this:

> There was fierce and almost cut-throat competition among the three so-called majority ethnic groups for federal hegemony. It was a war of giants for the waging of which the consent of the minority ethnic groups was never sought and, in any case, was taken for granted . . . Each of the three major ethnic groups regarded it as its destiny to lead the country, to the permanent exclusion of the other ethnic groups. In due course, this misguided ambition generated hatred among the three, fears, resentment and antipathy among the minorities and the pernicious disharmony among the entire group.[17]

As observed in Awolowo's submission, the major ethnic groups (Igbo of the southeast, Yoruba of the southwest, and the Hausa/Fulani of the north) all began to exert dominance over what they considered their domains. This meant the subjugation of smaller ethnic groups, and this was to draw reactions from the ethnic minorities as they feared possible marginalization and subordination.

Looking at the contemporary Nigeria, the body polity is impregnated by the teething problem of ethnicity. Since the return of the country to the path of democracy in 1999, most crises that have been taking place hinge strongly on ethnoregionalism. Chief Olusegun Obasanjo was often accused of implementing the Yoruba agenda during his tenure as the president of Nigeria from 1999 to 2007. About this time, the Igbos in the southeast had to renew their quest for secession as a result of the neglect of their homeland by the federal government. Later, the minority states of the oil-bearing south-south demanded resource control backed by militancy. The north was spoiling for violence as it sought to magnify its Islamic identity through the imposition of Sharia. And today, the Kanuri-dominated northeast is feeling marginalized and possibly serves a fertile ground for Boko Haram insurgency. A situation as this has been captured by Akinyele as he lamented that the ability of the government to deliver the dividends of democracy would, however, depend on the extent to which it is able to satisfy the political demands of the various ethnic groups.[18] This problem has contributed immensely in sparking violence that threatens to tear the country into shreds. In the next chapter, we are going to look at how various sections of the Nigerian state have been advancing ethnoregional militias in pursuit of the regional interest.

CHAPTER 3
Advancing Sectional Agenda through Ethnic Militias

As individuals crave for self-preservation, prestige, wealth, and total well-being, human groupings are not without similar cravings. More than three thousand ethnic groups in Nigeria are in intense competition for the pursuit of their aspirations. They need to preserve their existence, improve and sustain their distinct identities, be in control of power, gain an advantage in the allocation of resources, and ensure that they do not lose out or turn victims of uneven wealth distribution. In this scenario, clashes of interests are certain. When there is incompatibility of interests, conflicts set in and if not properly managed, escalate to the stage that induces violence. This explains why Nigeria is susceptible to ethnoregional-based violent conflicts. It is, therefore, the continued frustration of a certain group of people in pursuit of their aspiration in a highly pluralistic country that informs the need for self-help which turns out to breed militancy in various sections of the country.

There is hardly any conflicting issue in Nigeria without certain question arising to interrogate the ethnic source of players involved. Indeed, parties to conflicts can only enjoy fair judgment from the wider Nigerian public only if they all come from the same stock—that is, where actions and inactions could either be commended or condemned shorn of ethnic prejudice. Apart from this notion, every judgment is likely to be influenced on the basis of ethnicity. An ordinary, simple dispute involving parties from different ethnic groups is capable of escalating into serious violence that flows along ethnic course causing lives and properties to be lost wantonly. Therefore, when militant groups look out for targets outside their ethnic base, they tend to enjoy the support and sympathy of their fellow ethnics. In a country where the distribution of political power and socioeconomic resources are viewed under ethnic prism, suspicion remains constant. The slightest insensitivity or lopsidedness in resources distribution could induce armed struggle in such a way that what the conflicting parties lose, outweigh the gains they fought for. Therefore, in many sections of Nigeria where violent clashes are experienced, there is always a sharp fall in the human development index. Indicators such as lifespan, education, and per capita income reduce to a miserable low level. While indicators of human development gradually disappear in the face of armed conflicts, social maladies such as poverty, hunger, disease, illiteracy, and mortality rate, increase uncontrollably, thus keeping the country static at a level of enormous underdevelopment despite the huge natural resources available.

In a deeply divided country, such as Nigeria, ethnic affiliations as put by Donald Horowitz would only provide a sense of trust, certainty, reciprocal help, and protection. Such ethnic affiliations have naturally acquired greater salience and attraction as groups have increasingly found it necessary to mobilize against historical and contemporary iniquities and injustice in the sociopolitical process of heterogeneous state.[18] Thus, the Nigerian people are caught in between loyalty to the country and sympathy to the ethnosectional yearnings as manifesting in the formations of ethnic militias in recent history. In Nigeria, the love for one's country is suffocated by a concentric combination of ethnopolitical and geopolitical affiliation. Patriotism here is best described as painting a picture whereby loyalty for the polity starts from the ethnic environment. It further progresses to the state level, then extends to the region at large before eventually settling to the federation's plains. For example, a Yoruba man would see himself first as one of Yoruba ethnicity before thinking of themselves as belonging to Oyo, Ogun, Osun, Lagos, Ekiti, or Ondo State (Yoruba-dominated states). Thus, seeing themselves through the Yoruba lens magnifies the socioeconomic, political, and cultural supremacy of the southwest region. This tremendously matters to them much more than national aspiration. These folks would only see themselves as Nigerians when the country competes at an international level. The same illustration could be applied to an Igbo indigene, Ibibio indigene, Ijaw indigene, Itsekiri indigene, Urhobo indigene, Igala indigene, and a Tiv indigene. These indigenes inexorably also see themselves first as ethnic individuals before being considered as Nigerians. However, the case of the Hausas/Fulanis and Kanuris might be different because their identities hinged strongly on Islamic heritage. Here, as predominant Islamic adherents, loyalty to Islam is the foremost of all loyalties. Ethnic consciousness comes subsequently while patriotism for the country still trails behind. In a scenario such as this, the thought of national goals and aspirations becomes far-off in the face of ethnic yearnings. When ethnic agenda breeds militant insurgency, the fighters certainly enjoy massive support from their ethnic base while government forces lack support from the citizens in that same location.

In most cases, when the cooperation of members of the society is not forthcoming, out of frustration, the security forces would go on to unleash mayhem on the civilians. To justify the brutality, the victimized are criminalized or accused of aiding and abetting militants. When this happens, the militias would become extremely vindictive and stay passionate for vengeance.

The story of ethnoregional militias in Nigeria is the account of violent reaction of sections of the country towards oppression, marginalization, exclusion, the threat of genocide, religious domination amongst other anomalies. The country has witnessed national spread in the emergence of ethnic and regional militias, vigilantes, insurgents, and other armed groups. Although Nigeria has a long history of militancy, the rise of ethnic militias and vigilantes started to peak during late General Sani Abacha's military regime (1993–1998), a period where Nigerians experienced serious political deprivations and economic hardship. Beginning from the Yoruba-dominated southwest, the annulment of the June 12, 1993 elections by the military junta and the subsequent arrest and detention of Chief Moshood Abiola, a Yoruba man who was widely believed to have won the presidency in the annulled elections, sparked Yoruba ethnic sentiments, and O'odua People's Congress (OPC) was established in August 1994 to conquer what was alleged as the marginalization of the Yoruba people and to protect and defend the Yoruba ethnic interests. Although OPC's factional leaders—Dr. Frederick Fasehun and Gani Adams—had on several occasions claimed nonviolent stance, eyewitness testimonies in Lagos have confirmed that the OPC had used various forms of weapons ranging from firearms, machetes, daggers, knives, concentrated acid, petrol bombs, irons to massive sticks to wrought violence on non-Yoruba ethnics. There were cases where Yorubas were victimized as a result of factional clashes or perceived as working against the interests of the OPC and the collective ambition of the Yoruba group. At the same time OPC militias would brutally hack their victims to death and on occasion, pour acid on them. Corpses were set ablaze, and mutilation of bodies was also their stock in trade.

The major targets of OPC militias were Hausa elements and those suspected to be northerners living in the southwest. This came as a result of the usurpation of federal control by a northern military cabal. Although attacks were directed against Hausas, some Igbos, Ijaws, and other ethnic persons from the south-south were also harassed. OPC also clashed on several occasions with policemen. Notable incidences of violence were their engagement with the Hausa residents in Lagos at Ketu and Mile 12 Market in 1999. OPC also carried out bloody attacks in Shagamu in the year 2000.

Although the outrage against the annulment of the 1993 elections coupled with the contempt against repressive military regime acted as forceful drivers that prompted the formation of the militant group, the OPC was to adapt to the changing realities and the political dynamics. Its operations split into different directions ranging from agitation for

Yoruba political autonomy, promotion of Yoruba language and culture, violent struggles against other ethnic nationalities living in the southwest to vigilantism and the combating of crimes.

Olusegun Obasanjo's government was suspected to be lenient on OPC despite condemning its activities publicly. The group continued to enjoy massive support from influential government officials of Yoruba extraction. OPC members were seen providing security at public functions. The ethnic militant group enjoyed the support of Yoruba populace despite its violent tendencies. This ethnic consciousness, as expressed through OPC, lent motivation to other ethnic groups in the south-south, including the southeast. Since Lagos particularly was serving as the melting pot of Nigerian societies, the idea of using militias to articulate ethnoregional grievances easily diffused to other sections of the country, especially where there was brewing frustration.

Significantly, the Ijaws, Igbos, Urhobos, Itsekiris, Ogonis, Andonis, and several other ethnic minorities in the south-south could be said to draw inspiration from OPC and in so doing, came to organize their own version of militias in the Niger Delta region to help champion the cause for resource control and to achieve balance in the power equation of the country. In the north, as would be discussed later, Arewa People's Congress would be constituted in response to the massacre of the northerners in Lagos and other south-west cities and towns.

Moving to the southeast of Nigeria where Igbos are the predominant population, there emerged the Movement for the Actualization of the Sovereign State of Biafra (MASSOB).

The want of Biafra was informed by the feeling that the Igbos had been marginalized and excluded in the socioeconomic calculation as well as the political mainstream of the country. As captured by E. O. Nkolika in a paper presented at the third Global Conference on Pluralism, Inclusion, and Citizenship in Salzburg, Austria, in November 2007, "MASSOB claimed that the Nigerian state and its functionaries had systematically oppressed the Igbos since the end of the Civil War and sought to secure self-determination by resuscitating the Republic of Biafra, whose bid to secede from the federation was crushed by the Nigerian troops in 1970."[19]

Chief Olusegun Obasanjo was sworn into office as the president of Nigeria on May 29, 1999. In the few months that followed, Ralph Nwazurike and some Igbo elements stormed media houses in Lagos to announce the birth of MASSOB and the quest for the sovereign state of Biafra. Whether such move was motivated by the activities of OPC or outright reaction to the emergence of Obasanjo's presidency owing to his alleged role in the mass killing of Igbo civilians during the Civil War, the point here is that Igbos were also indirectly agitating for their own presidency in 2003, which was an electoral year. MASSOB threatened that nothing could stop Biafra from seceding by 2003 unless Nigeria produces a president of Igbo extraction. Although MASSOB claimed to be nonviolent, there were incidents of clashes with the government forces and victimization of other ethnic nationalities found in the southeast states. Given the wide support it received from Igbo populace, MASSOB became a strong influence in the region. For example, in August 2004, it was able to mobilize Igbo traders nationwide to stay away from markets.

MASSOB was also working side by side with the Bakassi Boys—a deadly Igbo militant group that mostly played vigilante role in the region. Bakassi Boys enjoyed popular support in the Igbo land where they operated. Their effectiveness was felt in the area of combating crimes and ridding southeastern cities such as Aba, Onitsha, and Owerri of armed robbery gangs. The Bakassi Boys were endeared to traders and residents and were supported by the governor of Abia State, Dr. Orji Uzoh Kalu, who later was accused by the political oppositions of using the vigilantes as a tool for intimidation.

In 2015, the Igbos in partnership with some ethnic minorities in the south-south were to express their sectional agenda when Dr. Goodluck Jonathan lost the presidency to General Muhammadu Buhari (Rtd.). They claimed that there was a conspiracy between the northern and southwestern cabals to deny their kinsman opportunity for a second term and viewed such as an act of marginalization calculated to keep the southeast and south-south regions at perpetual subjugation. Independent People of Biafra (IPOB) led by Mazi Nnamdi Kanu came out on this backdrop to agitate for the sovereign state of Biafra. The federal government alleged that the group was going violent and reacted swiftly by launching Operation Python Dance in 2017 in the southeast followed by the prescription of the group, and the leader vanished.

The south-south of Nigeria and by extension, the Niger Delta region had been the center of militant activities since the turn of the twenty-first century. Starting from when the country stumbled on crude oil in Oloibiri, in the present-day Bayelsa State, in 1958. Oil-bearing communities in the Niger Delta have continued to be described as poor, backward, and underdeveloped.[20] The federal government, backed by the Petroleum Decree of 1969, Offshore Decree of 1971, and Land Use Decree of 1978—has been receiving the highest percentage of oil profits without adequate provisions for the improvement of lives and infrastructures in the oil-bearing communities. As put by Udechukwu Udeke and James Okolie-Osemene, "The significant feature of the Niger Delta is the general state of underdevelopment, not only by world standard but by also in relation to many parts of the country."[21] Oil production and related activities have been causing serious ecological disruptions and environmental damage to the region, which takes a serious toll on agriculture. Indigenes suffer health problems as a result of environmental pollution. Another devastating consequence is the destruction of aquatic life in the area. Writing on dangers posed by oil production to marines in the Niger Delta, S. O. Aghalino and B. Eyinla stressed that in spite of the stupendous wealth Nigeria has generated from the production and sale of oil, one of the negative externalities from the oil industry is marine pollution occasioned by oil spillage and discharge of effluents.[22] The multinational companies operating in the region carry out their activities without adequately addressing the nagging problems of the indigenes through corporate social responsibilities. Oil companies, such as the likes of AGIP, Chevron, Elf, Exxon Mobil, Shell BP, and Texaco, would repatriate billions of dollars from oil profits to their home countries while about 50 percent of Nigeria's petroleum derivation would be distributed to non-oil producing northern states as federal allocation leaving the Niger Delta indigenes to grapple with their own problem of environmental degradation and infrastructural decay. While the degraded environment impeded agriculture, the region's crumbled infrastructure hampers the performance of its informal economic sector. There was also a growing sense of injustice and general feelings of deprivation when the indigenes of the region considered the enormous income the country generated from oil while they themselves were reduced to mere onlookers in the oil and gas sector. An argument arose that if about 95 percent of the country's income was generated from natural resource deposits in the Niger Delta, why were its indigenes living in extreme poverty, high rate of unemployment, and lacked the very basic necessities of life? This ignited a crisis which came into full effect as the indigenes of the oil-bearing region looked for another means to an end the perceived injustice.

It was the neglect on the part of the federal government to develop the Niger Delta despite the region's contribution of about 95 percent to Nigeria's foreign exchange earnings that prompted the springing up of militant groups in the Niger Delta. In the early period of the insurrections in 2006, the Movement for the Emancipation of the Niger Delta served as the umbrella organization covering several militant groups in the region. Some of the militias that demonstrated regional agitation include Egbesu Boys of Africa (EBA), the Federated Niger Delta Ijaw Communities (FNDIC), the Ijaw Youths Congress (IYC), Movement for the Survival of Ijaw Ethnic Nationality (MOSIEN), Ijaw National Council (INC), and other groups such as Niger Delta Peoples Volunteer Force (NDPVF), Movement for the Survival of Ogoni People (MOSOP), Niger Delta Liberation Front (NDLF), Joint Revolutionary Council, Niger Delta Vigilante (NDV), and the most recent ones, Niger Delta Avengers, Niger Delta Greenland Justice Mandate, Joint Niger Delta Liberation Force, amongst others too numerous to mention.

Niger Delta militants have been engaging government forces in fierce shooting combats both on land and in the creeks. They sometimes blow up and vandalize oil installations and take foreign workers hostage in an attempt to frustrate oil production.

Given the surge of militancy, civil agitations and increasing global attention on the region, the federal government of Nigeria under the leadership of late Alhaji Musa Yar'Adua set up the technical committee on the Niger Delta in September 2009. The committee was inaugurated by the former vice president, Dr. Goodluck Jonathan. The technical committee was tasked with the responsibility to collate and review past reports on the Niger Delta starting from Willink report. It is apt to note here that the Willink commission was set up by the British colonial government in 1957 with Henry Willink, Master of Trinity College, University of Cambridge, as its head. The committee was mandated to look into the minority fears of political domination.[23]

However, the forty-five-man technical committee on the Niger Delta came up with the recommendation of total amnesty for the militants as well as a process of demobilization, disarmament, and rehabilitation. It was also recommended that allocation of oil revenues to the region be increased, and the infrastructural development and human welfare services will be instituted.[24] Following this, President Yar'Adua offered amnesty to the repentant militants. They were rehabilitated, empowered, and reintegrated into the larger society. This would become a reference point whenever the question of dialogue with other ethnic militias from other regions arises, as it would be the case with Boko Haram insurgents in the northeast.

Arewa People's Congress (APC) formed in the northern region in 1999 by Sagir Mohammed, a retired army captain—was a reaction to the killings of northerners in Lagos and other southwestern towns and cities by OPC militants. Unlike other ethnoregional militias, APC was less violent. The group opted to look out for the excesses of the new Obasanjo's administration viewed by northerners as Yoruba's regime. As accounted by Moshood Omotosho, "APC claimed that the harassment of northerners in the Southwest was part of a Yoruba plan to secede and establish the O'oduwa Republic, that the then President of Nigeria, Olusegun Obasanjo was sympathetic to OPC's goals, and that the North would go to war if necessary to prevent national dismemberment."[25] In general terms, the aim of APC was to protect and safeguard the interest of the north wherever it is.[26] Unlike other militias that seek change, the Arewa People's Congress sought the maintenance of the status quo.[27] This helps buttress the claim that the north is more interested in one united Nigeria than other regions because it enjoys more benefits in the Nigerian project. This further accompanies the belief that given wide religious differences and cultural cleavages between the north and the south, the northerners would not have insisted on maintaining an undivided Nigeria if not for the availability of oil wealth in the Niger Delta down south.

Most northern cabals own oil blocs and head juicy political and government offices while enjoying massive remunerations derived from the oil proceeds which formed about 95 percent of the country's foreign earnings. Outside agriculture, the north is left with inconsequential sources of income. Therefore, the disintegration of Nigeria would not be in the regional interest of the north. The northerners would rather go to war in the event of a breakaway from Nigeria by their southern counterparts because such a move would basically constitute a threat to the very survival of the north. In this case, the APC's quest for unity came not because they so love and cherish one Nigeria, but for the fear of a doomed economy awaiting their region should the south go away with their oil wells.

Significantly, the mismanagement of the O'odua People's Congress's insurrection by the federal government, from the onset, had enabled the contagious spread of ethnoregional militancy in Nigeria. As a result of inefficient governance, sections of the country are opting for the use of violence with the justification that it is the only way their grievances could be heard. The southwest cultivated and groomed OPC for the advancement of its regional agenda; the Igbos of the southeast saw MASSOB, IPOB, and other groups as the teeth that could bite and secure them either the presidency or a sovereign state Biafra. In the south-south, militancy became a response to the grave injustice in the sharing of oil revenue between the federal government and the oil-producing states while the Arewa People Congress emerged in the north to maintain the hegemonic hold of the northerners over the rest of Nigeria. But there are the salient Kanuris in the northeast of Nigeria that are equally in need of emergence from the overbearing shadow of the northern Hausa/Fulani by any means, be it Boko Haram or anything else.

CHAPTER 4
Kanuri-Hausa/Fulani
Tension and Revolt Against Marginalization

Kanuri is the fifth largest ethnic group in Nigeria predominantly occupying northeast corner of the country. With pockets of population in some northern states, almost seven million Kanuri indigenes were reported in 2013 to live in Nigeria with over one million living in the southwest of the Republic of Chad. The southeast of Niger had close to nine hundred thousand Kanuri ethnics in its population while over fifty thousand were also reported to live in the northern Cameroons. Although the Kanuri is the predominant population in the northeast, there are enclaves of other ethnic minorities, including Hausa and Fulani elements in the region.

The Kanuris have had a glorious past. They are proud of a rich history. In about the nineteenth century, the Kanuris began a building process of an empire believed to be one of the oldest in the world. The empire, which flourished in the Lake Chad basin, has been described as one of the great crossroads of African culture and history.[27] It became the melting pot of several races from whom the Kanuri have emerged the most dominant group.[28]

For many years, according to F. K. Buah, what came to be officially known as the Kanuri Empire was made up of two parts separated by the lake. Kanem was in the east and Bornu on the west of the empire.[29] Kanem existed as the center of governance for many years, but in the fifteenth century, the seat of power was moved to Bornu.

The first known Mai (king) who ruled the early settlers was Dugu.[30] He founded the Sefawa dynasty believed to have lasted a millennium—certainly the longest in Africa. The Mai of Kanem established a center of power at N'jimi situated in the northeast of Lake Chad.

Although authors present conflicting dates on the start of Sefawa dynasty, the time would not be later than AD 774. The dynasty ended in 1846, and Shehu (Sheikh) dynasty took over, and it is still running at the time of this writing.

Kanuris were the earliest group in northern Nigeria to officially embrace Islam. It started when the tenth Mai called Umme Jilmi, who reigned from about 1085 to 1097, got converted to Islam. With the acceptance of the Islamic religion, Kanem Bornu became an influential Muslim empire. Umme's son Mai Dunama I succeeded him in 1097 and became a powerful king and a devout Muslim who made three important pilgrimages to Mecca. During his reign, as presented by F. K. Buah, "Islam began to exercise considerable influence on the social, political, and economic life of the growing Kanuri kingdom. Dunama I introduced into his kingdom a number of Muslim scholars and administrators who helped to run the empire."[31] He began to undertake territorial expansion and continued steadily until his death in 1150. Dunama II, an ambitious and warlike Mai, assumed the leadership of the empire and continued the agenda of territorial expansion. With a formidable cavalry of thirty thousand men, Mai Dunama II extended the empire to Fezzan in the north, Adamawa in the south, Bornu and Kano in the west, and Wadai in the east. The importance of this expansion was that it helped to spread Islam.[32] In fact, it was during the reign of Dunama II that the attempt was intensified in making Islam a state religion.

After the first Kanem-Bornu Empire that began in the nineteenth century came to an end in 1470 as a result of internal conflicts and tribal wars, the second took off immediately. Stability was restored to the Sefawa dynasty when Mai Ali Ghaji founded the second Kanuri Empire of Bornu with the seat of power at Ngazargamu. He enforced strict adherence to Islamic practices, such as Koran studies, and marrying of only four wives. According to Buah, as a fervent Muslim, Ali Ghaji made use of Islam as a unifying force, and Islamic laws and practices were introduced into the administration.[33]

Islam would become a defining factor that would condition the future of Kanuri-Hausa/Fulani relations and their neighbors. While the Kanuris had come in contact with Islamic religion as early as the eleventh century especially when Mai Umme Jilmi was converted to Islam in about 1090, the Hausa states were originally pagans until about fourteenth century when Sarki Yaji Ali, a Hausa king of the Kutumbawa dynasty who reigned from 1349 to 1384, embraced Islam. Muslim missionaries from Sankore (Timbuktu) in the north of Mali came to Kano, and Yaji with his subjects accepted Islam. Thus, a mosque was built in Kano, and consequently, Islam spread to other Hausa states. Katsina became the last Hausa state to accept Islam when it was converted in 1493 by a Muslim missionary from Egypt. There is another account that claims that Islam was introduced to Hausa from Bornu by Al-Maghili. This may be possible given the Kanuri regional dominance and early Islamic influence.

In Onwubiko's account, Islam was slow to take root among Hausas because the rulers and their subjects often went back to their old pagan ways.[34] It was in the first quarter of the nineteenth century, during the Fulani jihad that paganism gave way to fervent Islamism. The Fulanis who scattered all over western Sudan without a settled kingdom were believed to be among the group of people to embrace Islam early in West Africa. They became famous for their commitment to the Islamic faith, and wherever they were, they endeavored to present the purest form of Islam. Among them were great men of letters. For centuries, the Fulanis and many ordinary Hausa citizens or *talakawa* were subjected to oppression and heavy taxation imposed on them by the Hausa kings. In this regard, many Hausas were ready to join forces with the Fulanis in the struggle against their rulers. So when the Fulani jihad took place in Hausa in the nineteenth century, the oppressed were readily on the ground to support the crusade. The movement was led by an itinerant Fulani preacher and scholar Uthman dan Fodio, who was born in Maratta in Gobir in 1754. The aim of dan Fodio's crusade was to bring about far-reaching reforms in the religious system and to restore the pure form of Islam in the Hausa land.

Dan Fodio became so popular because of his anti-paganist campaigns, as well as his outbursts against the existing warped social order and political injustices, and he was seen as a threat by the monarch of Gobir. Tension brewed pitching Uthman dan Fodio against Yunfa who had been one of dan

Fodio's pupils that succeeded to the throne of Gobir in 1802. On February 21, 1804, Yunfa declared war on dan Fodio. Despite initial setbacks at Tsuntua and some other places, dan Fodio began taking over some important Hausa domains beginning from 1805. His forces were able to capture states of Katsina and Daura in 1807, and by 1808, the important kingdoms of Kano and Gobir were brought under dan Fodio's control.

Uthman dan Fodio's next move was to build a large empire where a purified form of Islam would be practiced. To achieve this aim, he gave flags of authority to his cronies, including some leaders of Fulani communities, and charged them to fight a holy war in their respective areas, and whoever succeeded was to become Emir and establish orthodox Islamic religion and government. In 1809, dan Fodio's son Muhammed Bello founded the city of Sokoto, which came to be the seat of Sokoto Caliphate.

The Fulanis turned their attention to Bornu in the east where they recorded temporary success. In 1808, when the Fulani jihadists attacked Bornu and sent away Mai Ahmad from N'gazargamu, a great Kanuri army commander and scholar from Kanem in the east crossed Lake Chad to beat down Fulani's offensive on the west. His name was Muhammad al-Amin Al-Kanemi. With his military and intellectual pedigree, Al-Kanemi was able to stand up against Fulani crusaders. Buah captured Muhammad Al-Kanemi's sagacity and gallantry in the struggle against the Fulani.

A devout Muslim, he adhered to a strict form of religion. He could, therefore, argue convincingly against Uthman dan Fodio, who claimed to be leading the Jihad against pagan territories. In correspondence with dan Fodio's son, Muhammed Bello, he argued against the intentions of the Fulani, saying that, far from adulterating Islam, Bornu practiced the purest form of faith, and therefore needed no external reformer.[35]

This marked a turning point in the Kanuri-Hausa/Fulani relations. When Mai Armad died, Al-Kanemi assumed the leadership of Kanem-Bornu Empire, replacing a thousand-year-old Sefawa dynasty with his own ruling line called *Sheikh* or *Shehu*, and the hostility deepened between the two blocs. Al-Kanemi died in 1835, but his ruling line still endures to this day.

The act of insulating the expansionist drive of the Sokoto Caliphate by Al-Kanemi's Bornu was not only bringing hostility between the two Islamic powers but to throw them into further rivalry in the areas of ideologies and Islamic literatures.

Given the foregoing, Sokoto Caliphate—a vast Fulani Muslim empire on Hausa land exists today side by side with the territory of former Bornu Empire which is now under the Sheik religious and traditional authority in northern Nigeria. As it stands, old Bornu is not taking directives from Sokoto Caliphate when it comes to religious, traditional, or cultural matters.

Although the British colonialists abolished the political authority of Sokoto Caliphate when they defeated it in 1903, the title of the sultan was spared, and it is still an important religious position for most northern Nigerian Muslims today. On the other hand, after the British expulsed Rabihaz-Zubayr who invaded Bornu in 1893, the declining empire was absorbed along with Sokoto Caliphate into a single geopolitical entity now called Nigeria.

Northern Nigeria today has presented a monolith outlook to outsiders in such a way that all northerners are erroneously referred to as Hausa/Fulani without regards to other ethnic identities. The Kanuri existence is seemingly eclipsed by the establishment of Sokoto Caliphate over the greater part of the northern region. Also, the emergence of Hausa as a lingua franca of the northern system has also helped in blunting the sharp edges of ethnic identities in the north. But for the fact that Kanuri-dominated northeast is not taking any directive from Sokoto Caliphate other than Shehu of Bornu shows a vital aspect of northern demarcation. In a way, the Kanuri group which had evolved a strong, vibrant empire long before the emergence of the Hausa/Fulani's Sokoto Caliphate does not seem to enjoy the current peripheral position it is being placed in northern and the Nigerian power game.

There is no doubt that the precolonial tension existing between the Hausa/Fulani's Sokoto Caliphate and Kanuri's Kanem-Bornu Empire has seeped through the colonial period down to contemporary Nigeria. Since Hausa/Fulani could not conquer Kanuri's Empire, postcolonial Nigerian state has offered the Hausa/Fulani majority the favorable apparatuses as well as anadvantageous environmental setting to dominate old Bornu area and silence the influence of Shehu's dynasty. The Nigerian security formations are dominated by Hausa/Fulani elements, and they are serving well enough the interests of Sokoto Caliphate. The era of military junta demonstrated this position. For example, as noted by R. T. Akinyele, "The unitary command structure of the military accentuated the lopsidedness of the distribution of the important political and military posts to the extent that the army was now regarded as the military wing of the Sokoto Caliphate."[36]

The late General Sani Abacha, a Kanuri from Kano State, had used his regime in an attempt to reverse the trend and to reposition Kanuri in Nigeria's power equation. Abacha retired several top military officers, many of whom were Hausa/Fulani. He also deposed the sultan of Sokoto Alhaji Ibrahim Dasuki, while the Shehu of Bornu, at the same time, was given prominence by his regime. But Abacha's endeavors could not bring up Kanuri to the core position of Nigeria's power domination.

Although Boko Haram was kick-started as an Islamic movement, it has now been conditioned by the naked threat of extermination to wear an ethnic garb. Since the majority of security operatives fighting Kanuri-dominated Boko Haram are of Hausa/Fulani extraction, the support of the Kanuri populace is unwavering for the militias. Support also comes from Kanuri descents living in the Niger Republic, Chad, and the northern Cameroons. Of course, nationals of the aforementioned countries were reported to have constituted the foreign elements among Boko Haram insurgents. Therefore, Boko Haram offers Kanuri ethnics a platform to square up against the menacing soldiers of Sokoto Caliphate hidden under the facade of Nigerian security to exterminate them.

In this connection, it is possible that Kanuri elements in

Nigerian security formations may have also contributed in no small measures in thwarting the effort of the government forces in furthering what they might have considered as ethnic cleansing. There have been allegations of security operatives working as secret informants within the ranks and files of Nigerian security system to keep Boko Haram leadership abreast of every plan and strategies concluded by government forces. And these informants may not be outside Kanuri stock. It has also been rumored that insurgents have been equipped with firearms and other weapons from government armories. If this is anything to go by, then the suppliers may be some Kanuri elements serving as Nigerian security operatives. It is not unlikely that they would be sympathetic to their kindred who have been killed, maimed, imprisoned, and abused by the military arm of Sokoto Caliphate working in the Nigerian security system.

Most of the Boko Haram worst hits had been carried out on non-Kanuri settlements to show that their operations are ethnic motivated. It seems like a fight for identity and self-preservation. Despite their glorious past, areas falling under the former Kanuri Empire in Nigeria are among the poorest states in the country. In terms of politics on the national front, they are increasingly losing out of the power game. Opening up in 2012, Barr. Ishaka Mohammed Bawa, a former chief whip in the federal house of representatives who also served as a house leader of the northeastern states' caucus said insecurity in the northeast region comes as a result of gross marginalization. According to him, "We felt that over the years, the Northeastern region had been marginalized in all aspects of life in this country, (and) marginalization is responsible for insecurity in the Northeast."[37]

Was marginalization the main foundation of Boko Haram insurgency and insecurity in the northeast? Well, a careful assessment may lead to the submission that the marginalization factor is just an afterthought when studying the evolution of Boko Haram. As you would come to comprehend, it started with Mohammed Yusuf, a Kanuri man who was exposed to Salafism and the teachings of Ibn Taymiyyah that espoused holy war against un-Islamic systems. When Yusuf formed Boko Haram, the bulk of his supporters were his fellow Kanuris. When he was eventually killed in Maiduguri along with some of his followers in July 2009 by security operatives, the immediate violent attacks launched by Boko Haram members were pure reprisal mission not insurrection of some sorts against marginalization. For the reason that many of the casualties were Kanuris, it became an ethnic reprisal under the mask of Boko Haram. The only reason these attacks were thought to stem from marginalization instead of direct vengeance was only adduced to rationalize the motive for brutality. If the Kanuris, ab initio, had intended to fight marginalization, then probably, it wouldn't have been through Boko Haram. It would have been through something else. In truth, Boko Haram militancy only sprang up out of some careless circumstances. Every indication points to this movement as one that was discovered, nurtured, and transformed by accident through an ethnic group who wanted reasons to justify their sectional agenda. This is not an attempt to relegate the marginalization factor to a state of irrelevance. Of course, there was marginalization which fertilized poverty in the northeast, and the people lived with the condition several years before Boko Haram militancy kicked off in 2009. There were no records of uprising connected with any case of marginalization. Today, even though the Kanuris see marginalization, poverty, poor infrastructural development, and political exclusion as grounds for insecurity in the northeast, there still exists an underlying religious wariness amongst the Kanuris over the Sokoto Caliphate's attempt to extend the Islamic dominance to the whole northern Nigeria. Note however that there is also a Christian factor to this puzzle by way of the increasing prominence of Christianity by the day in the Kanuri's sphere of influence or say the old Kanem-Bornu axis. This puzzle, the writer has deferred to the next writing series.

Many critics are of the opinion that poverty is the sole breeding factor of Boko Haram. The writer's take on this differs. Yes, poverty has catalyzed the already blown out situation, but on itself alone, it never was the fundamental factor for this insurgency. Note, however, that poverty is not only common in the eastern section of the north. Its tentacles have been spreading across northern Nigeria. Consider the fact that if poverty single-handedly bred Boko Haram insurgency, then the epicenter of the insurgency should have found a home in the northwestern or the north-central region where the rate of poverty skyrockets alarmingly to the high heavens. Reflect also on the fact that Boko Haram or an equivalent insurgency could have taken off anywhere in northern Nigeria if the only insurgency was a necessity to address the socioeconomic imbalance in the northern societies. It could have taken center stage at well-developed northern Nigerian states, such as Sokoto, Kano, Katsina, Gusau, or

Kaduna or anywhere in the rural northwest or north-central. The major role poverty plays in keeping alive the insurgency is by way of providing a huge reservoir of gullible youths where membership is drawn from to wage Kanuri insurrection.

The ethnic factor remains the mobilizing force that took advantage of the underclass poverty in the north as well as the perceived marginalization of the Kanuris to win converts for the Islamic militant group. In this light, marginalization and poverty have contributed immensely to deepening insecurity in the northeast even though there were not part of the central causes that gave rise to the insurrection. Other than being galvanized by the Kanuri factor, the Boko Haram insurgency would hardly have endured its many years of struggles with the federal security forces and wreacking unprecedented havoc on the socioeconomic environment of the Nigerian state.

CHAPTER 5
Evolution of Boko Haram
Story Behind the Story

The growth of Boko Haram insurgency in Nigeria is a story of radical Islamic ideas seized upon by violence, fueled by ethnic sentiments, galvanized by the quest for vengeance, and fed by political tendencies. Boko Haram offers many sides of a terror story in Nigeria. It is like a huge mountain at which individuals cannot picture all of it in a single view unless they hover above it. Many writers seem to look at the Boko Haram phenomenon from the sides instead of from the top to the base. Thus, its origin, growth, and magnitude to many discussants remain largely varied and inconclusive. Some writers single out certain factors as sparking off the insurgency. Such factors include Islamic extremism, poverty, illiteracy, unemployment, corruption, marginalization, and so on. But according to Nobel Prize winner, Professor Wole Soyinka, "To limit oneself to these factors alone, is an evasion, intellectual and moral cowardice and a fear of offending the ruthless caucuses that have unleashed terror on the society, a refusal to stare the irrational in the face and give it a proper name."

Indeed, the Boko Haram phenomenon in Nigeria is one that has made a mockery of scholars who thought they could unravel the mystery behind the insurgency without referencing ethnicity, which is the mother of all Nigeria's woes. When pointing to common factors that give rise to the crisis, it becomes pertinent to interrogate the subjects or the sources as the case may be. For instance, if a writer speculates Islamic radicalism as the cause of Boko Haram insurgency, the exploratory questions one should ask should aim to determine how large the number of Muslims that embrace radicalism is and how economically powerful they are to wage the so-called holy war against the larger society for almost ten years—and still counting. In another instance, if a writer declares the causative factor of Boko Haram to be poverty, can poor wages sustain such an expensive war for years against the government of the federal republic of Nigeria which has sufficient security personnel on the ground and enough weapons in its arsenal? If again, another writer points the root cause of this insurgency to lack of education and unemployment, then we will need to justify how illiterates can execute terrorism with immense sophistry or how a mass of jobless applicants can afford such a war. If we should then attribute the cause of this insurgency to corruption and marginalization, then it can begin to make more sense. Notwithstanding, the magnitude and the duration of the war will depend largely on what sides the corrupt take and the capability of the marginalizing elements to maintain the status quo. Taking this a step further, the author makes it clear that even though a deficient social system may have contributed immensely to the proliferation of this insurgency, the sustenance of this insurgency lies solely on ethnic factors being responsible for amplifying the Boko Haram militancy. This insight should directly pave the way for a solution in tackling the problem.

As we are going to find out, this narrative would not commit common errors by attributing the gamut of Boko Haram origin and evolution to a single factor. It would look at the stark realities and experiences surrounding Boko Haram; the environments that help the terrorist group develop to the level that reduces intellectual convictions to mere imaginations. Comparatively, Boko Haram is not like the O'odua People's Congress (OPC) founded on overt Yoruba assertiveness; it does not resemble the Niger Delta militants that built their existence around their ethnic positions and interests. Before making any attempt to compare Boko Haram with Arewa People Congress, it is necessary to note that the Arewas were, indeed, a mutant ethnoregional militia group which decided to weave northern interests into the Nigerian fabrics while carefully shying away from posing a disintegration threat to the country like their counterparts in other regions. In such respect, Boko Haram is not in the Arewa's mold. However, unlike other militias that developed with clear-cut objectives, Boko Haram emerged as a resultant combination of religious radicalization and vengeance for fallen members conditioned by the Kanuri factor (this includes the northern Nigerian system) in pursuit of fighting an eth-noregional cause which turned out to threaten the very existence of the Nigerian state.

Boko Haram's roots stem from ideas—some ideas founded many centuries ago outside Africa. The ideas that inspired the formation of Boko Haram lay in the teachings of a thir-teenth-century Sunni Muslim theologian, a legal scholar, a political theorist, and a logician. His name was Taqī ad-Dīn Ahmad Ibn Taymiyyah (January 22, 1263–September 26,

1328), shortened Ibn Taymiyyah. He came from Harran, east of Damascus. Forced by armed conflicts to leave his native Mongol country at the age of six, Ibn Taymiyyah took refuge in the territory of Bahri Mamluk Sultanate and was under the influence of Ahmad Ibn Hanbal.

As an Islamic fundamentalist, Ibn Taymiyyah detested the Mongol Muslims for observing Genghis Khan's Yasa codes instead of Islamic laws. He saw them as Kafr (apostates) believing that the Muslim Mongol leaders who refrained from implementing the Sharia were Kufr and not true Muslims, hence they objected to jihad. Since Kafr system was abhorrent to Ibn Taymiyyah, he saw jihad as a "decisive fight . . . against the disbelievers who are the enemies of Allah and his messengers." For the sake of Allah, Ibn Taymiyyah described jihad as "the best of all voluntary good actions which man performs . . . better than the grand pilgrimage."

In Ibn Taymiyyah's thinking, the ritual uniformity of all Muslim faithful was essential in fostering solidarity for piety and good deeds. Hence, he saw Mongol Kufr system as a contradiction to Islamic identity.

But Ibn Taymiyyah did not, in explicit terms, fashion out ways of waging jihad against the Kufr, although asserted that it is a personal duty on all to repulse the enemies if they decide to attack the Muslim faithful.

However, Ahmad Ibn Taymiyyah remained the medieval Islamic writer and theorist who strongly influenced contemporary Islam. Many radical Islamic scholars who look up to his teachings and Islamic movements, such as Salafism and Wahabalism, were strongly inspired by his works. In the late nineteenth century, the Salafist movement was developed in

Egypt as a reform branch of Sunni Islam apparently to insulate the European imperialism. The Salafist doctrine revolves around the concept of looking at the Salaf, who were the first three generations of scholars after Prophet Muhammad. The Salafists believe that the contemporary world could only be ordered and understood if the faithful return to life prior to the historical period. Salafism rejects innovation in Islamic system (bid'dah) and supports the implementation of Sharia. They strongly push for advocacy for the return of the Salaf traditions. The movement consists of the purists who stay away from politics, the activists who involve in political activities, and the jihadists who espouse holy war against supposed enemies of Islam.

The teachings of Ibn Taymiyyah and Salafism would become the major forces combined to influence the thinking of Mohammed Yusuf, a Kanuri from northeastern Nigeria. Born on January 29, 1970, in a village called Girgir in Jakusko, in the present-day Yobe State, Mohammed Yusuf was claimed to have studied theology in the University of Medina in Saudi Arabia. Young Yusuf was inspired by Ibn Taymiyyah's theories and was instructed in Salafism. A key Salafist scholar and leader who also won Yusuf's admiration was Shukri Mustafa, an Egyptian who preached religious intolerance and founded an Islamic sect in the 60s known as Salafist Takfir wal-Hijra movement which indulged in fighting other Islamists they deemed apostates. This background had a defining impact on Mohammed Yusuf's thinking as he would look for a way to topple the Kufur system in Nigeria.

Around 2002, Mohammed Yusuf founded an Islamist group with the official name *Jama'atuAhlis Sunna Lunna*

Lidda'awatiwal-Jihad, meaning "people committed to the propagation of the prophet's teachings and jihad." The group is known popularly as *Boko Haram.* Yusuf established a mosque in Maiduguri named after Ibn Taymiyyah.

According to Tajudeen Akanji, Boko Haram, as an Islamic sect, "believes northern politics has been taken over by a group of corrupt and false Muslims. It wants to wage a war against them and the Federal Government of Nigeria in general, to create a "pure" Islamic state ruled by Sharia." The sect viewed coeducational school as breeding prostitution among the youths. They questioned some scientific theories that tend to contradict Islamic beliefs and scriptural claims. As Akanji noted, "Issues like Evolution Theory, the round shape of the earth which they claim is flat, and the source of rainfall which they believe is the work of the Angels are central in their contestations with Western epistemology." In an interview with BBC in 2009 captured by Wikipedia, Mohammed Yusuf said the following:

> There are prominent Islamic preachers who have seen and understood that the present Western-style education is mixed with issues that run contrary to our beliefs in Islam.
>
> Like rain. We believe it is a creation of God rather than an evaporation caused by the sun that condenses and becomes rain.
>
> Like saying the world is a sphere. If it runs contrary to the teachings of Allah, we reject it. We also reject the theory of Darwinism.

Presenting a linguistic explanation to the meaning of Boko Haram, Professor Abdulla Adamu of Bayero University in Kano presented in a lecture delivered at NIPPS, Jos in 2012.

> Technically, 'boko haram' means 'deceptive knowledge which is sinful,' not Western education is sin.' This is because charlatan marabouts—basing their epistemology on a faulty interpretation of Islamic injunctions to deceive clients—are also technically 'yanboko' (dispensers of deceptive knowledge).

Professor Adamu also averred that the major intention of Yusuf's teachings and texts was to convince his followers that knowledge inspired by Western ideals is false in some respects, but neither he nor his followers ever actually proclaimed that such knowledge is sinful. This position may be supported by local rumors that Yusuf lived a lavish lifestyle using Western items, like mobile phones including the possession of a Mercedes-Benz. In this light, Professor Abdulla Adamu believed that the view that the sect abhorred Western education in totality was the process of demonizing the movement, hence the creation and projection of medieval persona of the group as condemning Western education— which is the fact the sect found amusing since they not only use products of Western technology and knowledge, like laptops, arms, explosives, but at one stage had a full-blown website that proclaims their ideals.

Akanji writes that Boko Haram initially resolved to wage jihad against bad governance, official immorality and obnoxious modernity teachings. Despite its militant outlook, the initial methodology adopted for propagation was relatively nonviolent. Accordingly, as reported by Agence Presse in January 2006, Mohammed Yusuf was quoted the following:

> I think that an Islamic system of government should be established in Nigeria and if possible, all over the world, but through dialogue.

But the incident on June 11, 2009, would change the life and character of the Islamic sect which in turn would throw the country into the precarious security situation. On the aforementioned date, the security operatives raided a funeral procession of the sects. The mourners, who were on motorbikes, had refused to put on crash helmets as required by law. Consequently, the members of the anti-robbery joint task force comprising of military personnel and policemen opened fire on the procession which caused close to twenty deaths on the side of the sects. As noted by Tajudeen Akanji, the leader of the sect was reported to have written an open letter to the Nigerian president, seeking charges to be laid against the killers of his followers. Instead, what followed was the hounding of his followers by the security operatives. Yusuf was reported to have released several video messages where he urged his members to take up arms against the government of Nigeria.

In response to the call to violent retaliation, the group took to the streets of Maiduguri, attacking police stations and security operatives. Innocent members of the public were indiscriminately murdered in the process. In reaction, the security apparatus set in place to counter the uprisings called *Operation Flush* comprising of the military, police, and some other personnel. They were reinforced, and they clamped down on Boko Haram suspects and sympathizers. As accounted by Akanji, "Dozens of people were rounded up and executed without trial, including Yusuf's father-in-law, Muhammed Fugu, who, in fact, was not part of the group." Joint military task force engaged in excessive use of force, physical abuse, secret detentions, extortion, burning of houses, stealing of money during raids, and extrajudicial killings. It was this brutal response of the government forces that prompted Yusuf to declare war on the people of Nigeria saying in a leaflet, "*in mayeya manta,*" meaning if perpetrators have forgotten, the victims will not.

But who were the victims? They were majorly the Kanuri people. They had suffered the scorching rage of the Nigerian forces dominated by Hausa/Fulani and other ethnic elements. Kanuri victims had lost their loved ones, their houses burnt, and relatives detained without trial. Boko Haram gained support and sympathy of the Kanuri populace, and the recruits joined the militia not purely because of Islamic reasons but based on sheer ethnic sentiments and quest for vengeance. Apparently, the Kanuri's saw nothing good in Nigeria except endemic poverty and marginalization of their region. Notably, the Kanuris have equally fallen victim in the hands of Boko Haram militants. Yes, they have! Those perceived to have partnered with the government to work against the mission of the insurgent group are not spared. They are witch-hunted, fished out, and hacked to death. Even the Shehu of Bornu, the highest traditional authority in the Kanuri land who seemed not to favor the insurgency, was reported to have been targeted by the insurgents. There were other cases where notables of Kanuri extraction in the northeast were rounded up and killed because of their indifference or support for the status quo antebellum.

Following the uprising, Yusuf was captured by the army at his parents-in-law's house and handed over to the police. The police summarily executed Yusuf outside the police headquarters in Maiduguri on July 30, 2009. This was followed by claims that he died because of the severe pains emanating from injuries he sustained in a battle with the army. Reprisals were to follow Yusuf's death in alarming proportions.

After Yusuf's death, his right-hand man, Abubakar Shekau— a Kanuri from Yobe State—took on the mantle of Boko Haram authority. With his accession to leadership, the insurgents' attacks increased both in frequency and sophistication. The group became more organized in its approach to terrorism. The insurgents killed tens of thousands of people consisting of both security personnel and the civilians.

Galvanized by vengeance, Boko Haram soon metamorphosed from a pure Islamic movement to an organization executing ethnoregional and political agenda. The high-profile assassinations of political office seekers were perpetrated prior to 2011 elections in Borno State. For example, governorship aspirants, like Alhaji Awana Ngala and Alhaji Modu Fanami Gubio, were assassinated. Alhaji Lawan Yaraye and Alhaji Fannami Ngarannani, former local government council chairmen, were all murdered by Boko Haram for purely political reasons. After the swearing-in of President Goodluck

Jonathan, a Christian from southern Nigeria, at an event that took place in Abuja on May 29, 2011, the insurgents there and then carried out bombings in Abuja and Bauchi, killing about fifteen people. This was followed by the bombing of the United Nations headquarters in Abuja on August 26, 2011, where over twenty people were feared to be dead. The incident announced strongly to the world the presence of a deadly terrorist group domiciled in Nigeria.

Since the Kanuris, a predominant ethnic group in the northeast had no mechanism set in place to help in advancing their sectional agenda, Boko Haram became a readily available tool in that regard. With Boko Haram, the age-long, cooled ethnoreligious animosities would be heavily reignited. Reminisce that while the Kanuris precolonial Islamic and territorial expansion was overtaken by Sokoto Caliphate on the west, some troublesome ethnic minorities in the south blockaded them on their way to take Islam southward towards the Niger-Benue basin. Whereas various non-Kanuri ethnic minorities occupying the southeastern part of the present-day Borno State had enjoyed a considerable level of autonomy prior to the colonial era, they stiffly resisted Kanuri Muslim and Fulani slavers. They even enjoyed the liberty to practice Christianity, including syncretism, but lo and behold would suffer the onslaught of the Kanuri-controlled militia, Boko Haram.

Gwoza, a multilingual local government area in southern Borno State, had faced the threat of ethnic cleansing in the hands of Boko Haram. On February 15, 2014, Boko Haram murdered about 106 people in the mostly Christian dominated village of Izghe and later burned down the village to the ground. Additionally, over two thousand, mainly boys and men who were predominantly Christians, were massacred in Gwoza by the insurgents on June 2, 2014, after they assassinated Idrissa Timta, the Emir of Gwoza, two days earlier.

On February 14, 2014, the Christian population was targeted by Boko Haram in Konduga, southeast of Maiduguri, where about 120 were killed. Konduga has Shuwa Arab, Kanuri, Wandala/Malgwa populations, and other ethnic minorities. When considering the ethnic composition of the casualties, it is likely the majority of the victims would be non-Kanuri elements. The Margali and Fulani populations in Borno and Adamawa living close to Cameroon borders also formed part of Kanuri militants' targets.

Most of the areas occupied by minority ethnicities were annexed and declared Boko Haram caliphates by Abubakar Shekau, the Boko Haram leader, but were later recovered by the Nigerian military forces.

On April 14, 2014, Chibok, a non-Kanuri Christian town in southern Borno, suddenly came into international limelight. About 276 female students were kidnapped by Boko Haram insurgents at the Chibok government school. The girls, most of whom were Christians, were forcefully converted to Muslims as evidenced in a video released by Abubakar Shekau. The insurgent continued to ravage the northeastern part of the country with a series of massacres and large-scale abductions.

From a humble beginning, Boko Haram has won international recognition as a terrorist group. Claims are widespread that they have formed an alliance with al-Qaeda and the

Islamic State of Iraq and Syria (ISIS) / Islamic State of Iraq and the Levant (ISIL) terrorist groups in the Middle East. Notwithstanding, it is important to note that Boko Haram insurgents no matter the religious agenda it claims to pursue, is deeply watered by the Nigerian factor of ethnicity and steered by ugly northeastern politicking.

CHAPTER 6
Resisting Boko Haram Insurgency
Dangers of Using Force, Fear of Direct Dialogue

Humans have a common tendency in a violent scenario. They think vengeance whenever they see their family members, relatives, or loved ones lying in the pool of blood. The only form of justice thinkable becomes, naturally, spilling of blood for the shed blood. Some sympathizers that join the battle do so not with recourse to the root cause of the matter but out of a sheer quest for vengeance. If the offensive side increases the velocity of the attacks, correspondingly, the fury and aggression on the victims' side would also escalate in tempo either to achieve parity or win the odd. One of the fundamental conditions that precipitated different sections of Nigeria into a situation of wanton violence is the government's excessive use of force to quell uprisings. Barr. Kayode Oladele, the president of the justice center in Detroit, USA, in his paper presented in 2004 in Bremen, Germany, on ethnic militias in Nigeria captured succinctly the poor attitude of Nigerian government and security forces in the face of upheavals.

> The Nigerian government's human rights record remains very poor and in most cases, represents a violation of the Universal Declaration of Human Rights of which Nigeria is a signatory. The police, military,

and security forces continue to commit extrajudicial killings and use excessive force to apprehend and to quell several incidents of ethno-religious violence. The security operatives oftentimes beat, flog, torture and kill detainees and peaceful protesters. In most cases, neither the police nor the military were held accountable for excessive use of force or the death of members of these militia organizations. Cases of arbitrary arrest and detention of members of militia organizations remains a serious problem in Nigeria.

The leader-follower relationship in Nigeria is yet to overcome the hangover of the military junta. Power class expects the government to always remain docile, stay biddable, and dance to every whim. Where there is instability, there is that tendency on the part of the government to use coercion to enforce compliance. In Nigeria, there are several cases where those in authority would direct security forces to disperse peaceful protesters. Most at times, events of civil unrest are first responded through the use of coercion before getting the parties in conflict to the table. Normally, this happens after colossal bloodshed and wanton destruction of properties. In a situation where the relationship between the leadership and followership in a democratic setting looks more of a master-slave union in nature, there's bound to be leadership's abuse of power and security clampdown on dissenters. This background accounts for numerous clashes between government forces and those that challenge the status quo.

The federal government of Nigeria has quite a record of

criminalizing the demand of ethnic militias, including indis-criminate use of coercion to enforce social order under its belt. Kayode Ogundamisi who served as OPC's national secretary revealed in January 2000 that "over 1,800 OPC members were being detained without trial, with many killed, while homes of Yoruba were illegally raided by security agents." According to human rights world report, "police raids for suspected members of the OPC resulted in the arbitrary detention of hundreds of people and summary exe-cution of dozens." In February 2001, the security operatives killed ten people and destroyed the Movement for the Actu-alization of the Sovereign State of Biafra (MASSOB) head-quarters in Okigwe. The following year, MASSOB leader, Ralph Uwuzurike, claimed that one thousand MASSOB members remained in detention without charge in Umuahia, Abia State. In the Niger Delta region, scores of Odi community indigenes were massacred on November 20, 1999, by the military, and houses were set ablaze in response to the alleged killings of policemen in the community. This also contributed in forcing the youths of the area to embrace mil-itancy as a way of expressing the grievances.

Cases of government high-handedness in managing crisis situations in the country are numerous. Experience has shown that instead of de-escalating the crises, the government's extreme combative approach usually aggravate the situation causing irreparable loss of human lives and properties and it becomes more serious when ethnic sentiment is wiped into the matter. We can see how Boko Haram got transformed from a nonviolent movement to a dreadful militant group with a penchant for bloodletting, owing to governments mismanagement of the conflict at the initial stage. Notably, Boko Haram was founded in 2002 and did not involve in serious violent activities for about seven years after it was set up. The June 2009 killings of the sects at a burial function of a Boko Haram member by the government's anti-robbery task force drew the ire of the Islamic sects. In reprisal attacks that followed, the group saw their leader, Mohammed Yusuf, lose his life while in the custody of the Nigerian police force. This would mark a watershed in the history of terrorism in Nigeria.

The federal government has adopted several counter-insurgency and counter-terrorism measures to stem the tides of insecurity in the northeast, but sadly, peace still remains far from the horizon. Back in 2007, government stationed *Operation Flush* to contain the possible uprising in the northeast. Later, when the sect's new leader Abubakar Shekau took the insurgency to a virulent phase, the federal government under Dr. Goodluck Jonathan mobilized arm forces totaling one hundred thousand personnel to confront the insurgents in the northeast. In May 2013, the federal government declared a state of emergency in Adamawa, Borno, and the Yobe States. The Seventh Division of the Nigerian army was positioned in Maiduguri to take the fight to Boko Haram militants in their enclaves. In providing legal backing to the war against terrorism, an Anti-terrorism Act was passed. According to a statement released by Reuben Abati, the media and publicity adviser to President Goodluck Jonathan, the federal government formally approved the proscription of Boko Haram and authorized the gazetting of an order declaring the insurgents' and terrorists' activities illegal. The order gazetted as the Terrorism (Prevention) (Proscription Order) Notice affects both Boko Haram (Jama'atu Ahlis-Sunna Liddaawatiwal Jihad) and its faction Jama'atu Ansarul Muslimina Fi Bihadis Sudan. This was approved by President Goodluck Jonathan in pursuant to section 2 of the Terrorism Prevention Act, 2011 (as amended). The Act stipulated, amongst other provisions, a death penalty for the insurgents and destruction of their domains. Here, it is worthy of note that former President Olusegun Obasanjo in the spirit of government's custom of crushing the uprising with force presented a bill on April 9, 2002, to the national assembly prohibiting ethnic militias and related groups. The bill provided that no group of persons, association of individuals, or quasi-military group shall retain, organize, train, or equip any person or group of persons for the purpose of enabling the group of persons or association of individuals to use or display physical force or coercion in order to promote any political objective or interest, ethnic or cultural interest, social, occupational or religious interest. Obasanjo's bill prescribed a punishment of five years for individuals who violate the provisions of the proposed law and a fine of N 500,000.00 for corporate bodies. Although the bill was not passed into law, the federal government continued to employ coercion in quelling insurrections everywhere in the country.

As per Boko Haram, since the majority of the insurgents are of Kanuri extraction, the ethnic group has gotten the full wrath of the Nigerian government. There is, probably, a certain high degree of Kanuri's resentment of the Nigerian state as they lose their kindred on a regular basis to war against terrorism. The more the federal government use coercion to enforce peace, the more the antagonism of Kanuris against the government intensifies, and the more Boko Haram militants steadfastly defy all measures aiming at bringing peace to the war-torn region. They unrelentingly attack soft targets to harass Nigerians and to unsettle the arm forces.

Indeed, the Nigerian government's single-mindedness in using force to silence insurrections has badly backfired in an attempt to resist Boko Haram insurgency. The peace-at-all-cost campaign in the northeast laid more emphasis on the use of force. On July 19, 2015, at Konduga in Borno State, when the chief of army staff Major-General Tukur Buratai was changing the code of military operation in the northeast from "operation zaman lafiya" translated from Hausa as "let peace reign" to "*Operation Lafiya* Dole," meaning "peace at all means." The use of more to achieve peace became overt in Burutai's speech. In his words, he said the following:

> We are here to bury the "Operation Zaman Lafiya" and give birth to what we will henceforth call Operation Dole . . . *Operation Lafiya Dole* is derived from the belief that we must end this insecurity. We must restore peace to all parts of the Northeast and other parts of the country that are affected by insurgency.

He further added the following:

> As the insurgents have refused to understand and

come the right way, we must force them to make sure that peace return to all parts of Nigeria.

One fact to note here is that emerging victorious in a war is possible, but winning peace can be very expensive and difficult. Given Buratai's declaration above, how many suspected insurgents would the Nigerian government forces have to kill in order to restore peace in the northeast? How many houses would they torch down to force the militias to succumb? How many thousands more suspected Boko Haram insurgents would the security operatives have to detain in a bid to enforce peace? How many suspects would the army subject to abuse and torture so as to restore order to the devastated region?

If *Operation Lafiya Dole* succeeded in killing thousands, destroyed houses, detained a lot of suspects, and tortured them severely, would all that effort compel Boko Haram to surrender? Even though they capitulate to ceasefire, would that guarantee peace? When the thought of killing the defiant insurgents came, did *Operation Lafiya Dole* also think about the vast number of the bereaved that it would create? Fathers and mothers, probably, would lose their children and vice versa; violent death would separate spouses and siblings; dependents would lose their breadwinners, and there would be a massive loss of jobs. In a situation as such, where is the place for peace for individuals who lost their loved ones? When the supposed productive segment of the population is bled out and the economic pattern of the affected societies disrupted by coercive activities of *Operation Lafiya Dole,* where would peace find its place in the midst of despair and soaring poverty? When houses are set ablaze, would peace be possible at a place where there is vast numbers of internally displaced persons? The bottom line is that *Operation Lafiya Dole* may succeed in restoring temporary calm. However, it may be unable to win the peace in a situation where families are massively bereaved, vast numbers internally displaced, a number that continues to rise at an alarming scale. It seems rather difficult to achieve peace in a society where there is biting hunger, abject poverty, and deprivations of the basic necessities to life. The managers of the *Operation Lafiya Dole* might have forgotten that peace is not just an absence of war, rather a sum total of all elements of human welfare and human harmony with their environment. Peace has to do with the protection of family life; it has to do with the availability of food, access to clean water, good healthcare system, electricity, quality education for young people, job opportunities, justice, fairness, and respect of fundamental human rights. When coercion is employed to enforce peace at all cost, it ends up creating deep resentment and defiance with all amount of determination aimed at thwarting the peace effort.

In December 2016, President Muhammadu Buhari announced the final crushing of Boko Haram terrorists in their last enclave. In response, Abubakar Shekau, in a video, declared a renewed war on the country, urging his followers to "kill all the infidels and detonate bombs everywhere. Yes! I want you to kill, slaughter, and abduct."

Following Shekau's declaration, Boko Haram in January 2017, carried out twin bombings at the University of Maiduguri, sacked Dzaku village in Askira-Uba local government area of Borno State, killing eight and kidnapped both women and children. In February of the same year, the Islamic militants launched an attack on a military base and went ahead to burn down Sasawa, a town near Damaturu, the Yobe State capital. In Borno, seven soldiers of *Operation Lafiya* Dole died after the troop fell into Boko Haram ambush in Ajiri community in Dikwa local government area. In July 2017, Boko Haram launched a suicide bombing attack on two internally displaced persons (IDP) camps in Maiduguri, killing about seven persons. They attacked an oil exploration team in the Magumeri area of Borno State, killing at least sixty-nine people including soldiers and civilians. Boko Haram attacks in 2017 alone were responsible for the death of more than two hundred people. That year suicide bombing increased in scale, dozens were abducted, and properties were destroyed despite the "peace by all means" mechanism set in place to end insurgency and terrorism in the northeast.

Nigerians had become weary of the protracted insurgency, and stakeholders had consistently called on the federal government to consider dialogue as a veritable tool to the solution of the insecurity in the northeast. But the federal government would not compromise with its position of non-dialogism because succumbing to the demands of the terrorists would show the weakness of the federal government in providing adequate security to its citizens. Indeed it is a common policy of most governments in the world, especially those in the West not to negotiate with the terrorists. On June 18, 2013, G8 leaders comprising of Canada, France, Germany, Italy, Japan, United Kingdom, United States, and the European

Union signed an agreement against paying ransoms to terrorists as they would understand that there would be no reward in trading hostages. There is, certainly, a good argument that should governments pay the ransom, it would inspire criminal-minded elements to go on a kidnapping spree, thus finding terrorism a very lucrative venture.

According to Peter Neumann, the argument for not negotiating with terrorists is simple. Terrorists must be rewarded for using violence. By negotiating with terrorists democracies lend legitimacy to terrorists and undermine groups which have pursued political change through peaceful means. Peace talks can destabilize the negotiating system political systems, undercut international efforts to outlaw terrorism, and set a dangerous precedent.

But in practice, democratic governments often dialogue with the terrorism. Rumors were rife that President Buhari's government despite vowing not to sit down at the round table with the terrorists had clandestinely negotiated with Boko Haram for the release of Chibok school girls that were kidnapped in April 2014 as well as Dapchi female students in Yobe State carted away by the insurgents in February 2018. The question is if the federal government had negotiated to achieve a partial objective, is it not the same as dialoguing to achieve total peace?

Amnesty for the Niger Delta militants had set precedence, whereby many commentators mostly referred to when searching for solutions to Boko Haram insurgency. President Umaru Yar'Adua in August 2009 offered an unconditional pardon and money to militants who agreed to lay down their arms and ammunition. The government announced that the gunmen who surrender their weapons would be given about £255 a month in cash and food allowance during the rehabilitating period. The militants, surprisingly, came out from the creeks to embrace this peace initiative. To some commentators, this approach could have also been adopted in finding a solution to the insurgency razing the northeast. However, they fail to consider the fact that the root cause of militancy in the Niger Delta is quite different from the one that sprouted insurgency in the northeast. In the case of Niger Delta, poverty, unemployment, and infrastructural decays all formed the unequivocal reasons for the unrest as voiced out by the militants. But in the northeast, the abstract religious beliefs are presented as the basic cause of the insurrection while the main problems of ethnic socioeconomic and political imbalances lurk beneath the surface. Therefore to offer a solution to the insurgency, the first activity becomes unmasking Boko Haram's religious ugly face to bare the fundamental problems plaguing the Northeast.

For the fact that most of Nigeria's crises hinge on ethnicity, negotiating with Boko in order to end the northeast turmoil would create more unrests in the country sooner than later. Various militias representing different sections would emerge across the country, sorting after militancy and terrorism as the best of all methods in advancing their grievances to get a fair share of the national cake for their ethnic and regional groupings. If the federal government directly negotiates with Boko Haram insurgents, it, therefore, implies that Nigeria would have more militants and terrorists to negotiate with in the future.

Looking at the composition and texture of the Boko

Haram problem, the solution is neither the use of force nor direct dialogue. The continued use of force would add more fuel to the fire, and the dialogue with the insurgents might temporarily end the problem of insecurity in the northeast but would give birth to similar troubles all over the country in the future given Nigeria's common problem of ethnic suspicion. This is not to say that insurgency in the northeast would die a natural death. It is to suggest that the path to take in ending the insurgency begins with tackling the Kanuri question from inside out.

CHAPTER 7
Ending the War
Kanuri as a United Front

To end the war, peace brokers must first look at the crisis through the Kanuri eyes. This is not to rationalize the annoying violence and criminalities that has ravaged the northeast but to reconstruct the circumstances that amplified the unrest in the region. Looking away for a moment at the alleged religious foundation of the crisis, the first move to consider in a bid to disentangle the northeast from the deadly grips of insurgency and terrorism is to understand how one feels, seeing loved ones die gruesomely, their houses burnt down mindlessly, and wealth which took years to acquire being destroyed in one fell swoop by security operatives. Peace brokers must first imagine the pains Kanuri locals feel and their resentment towards the constituted authority in the whole Boko Haram debacle. Adopting this standpoint means looking at the problem from inside out. Since Boko Haram militants are not sustaining the war at their own cost but largely dependent on the sponsorship and resources of individuals and groups in the larger society, those interested in resolving the crisis need to personalize the motivations of sponsorship and encouragement of Boko Haram militancy. This is the first step to go and a sure way to cure the menace of its root.

This is however not an attempt to dictate to the decision

makers how to permanently resolve the Boko Haram troubles but to unveil a perspective that could possibly provide inroads to the peaceful ending of the insurgency without the federal government necessarily compromising with her national pride or hurting the ego of the Kanuris. It is to look for an alternative way to the use of force in suppressing the insurgency, while, at the same time, avoiding a direct dialogue with the Boko Haram militants for fear of creating a dangerous precedent. The bottom line is that the war may come to a close if the Kanuris are given a voice, at which point, we get them to unanimously say, "it is over!"

In other parts of Nigeria where ethno-based crises held sway, socio-cultural arrangements helped articulate the needs of the conflicting parties. They lend a voice that spell out the position of the aggrieved and would use the same voice to call the combatants to order in the language they understand. As noted in the early chapters of this book, the Ibibio State Union, a foremost sociocultural organization in the country, was very active in ending the Aba Women's Riot of 1929. Another instance was the role of Afenifere during Ife crisis in March 2017. As would be noted, Afenifere, a well-known pan-Yoruba sociocultural organization, has been a formidable force standing in the gap to protect the Yoruba interests, preserve their ethnic identity, and act as a voice in times of crises in the southwest region. In the ethnic conflict that sparked off on March 8, 2017, in Ile-Ife, Afenifere exerted the strong influence which insulated the aggression that could have balled the crisis out of control. The incident was caused by an altercation between a Yoruba woman by the name Kabura and a Hausa man. The incident happened at the Sabo area of the city which led to the stabbing of the woman's husband—a situation that escalated to killings and wanton destruction of properties. In the ensued crisis that pitched the Yorubas against Hausas/Fulanis, Afenifere vowed to resist the undue deployment of the federal government's might to settle ethnic scores. Instead, they chose a peaceful, legal angle promising to provide sufficient legal representation to defend close to twenty-one suspects of Yoruba descent, arrested by the police in connection to the crisis. In a statement released by the apex Yoruba group, they cautioned the police to live above board in dealing with a situation of such nature by refraining from engaging in actions that might trigger another crisis in the society. The group maintained that "Hausas and Yorubas have been living together in Ile-Ife and other towns in Osun State for a very long time, and the avoidable Ile-Ife crisis should not be allowed to escalate."

Similarly, in the second week of September 2017, the whole country was at the verge of falling into full anarchy and chaos when a report surfaced alleging the killings of the northerners by members of the Independent People of Biafra (IPOB) in the southeast and the south-south region of the country. Surprisingly, there was unusual self-restraint exercised by the northerners during the period which was made possible by the Arewa Youth Forum (AYF), a youth wing of the Arewa Consultative Forum in the north. Alhaji Gambo Ibrahim Gujungu, the AYF president, said he and the members of the forum's national executive council had sleepless nights engaging other youth associations across the north to ensure that there was no reprisal attack. On the other hand, the southeast group, the Ohanaeze Ndigbo, had to enter into an agreement in Abuja with leaders of other ethnic nationalities to promote peace and ensure the safety of every Nigerian while lending support to the decision of the southeast governors to proscribe IPOB. Also, the Ohanaeze Youths Congress (OYC) in a statement signed by its president, Mazi Okechukwu Isiguzoro, and other executive members noted that before the launching of Operation Python Dance 2 to quell IPOB activities in the southeast, there was already a reasonable level of discussion between OYC and IPOB.

Note also, the ex-militants in the Niger Delta that were given presidential amnesty in 2009, at some point, have been serving as a strong voice in their region as well as a mediatory factor in the numerous crises scenario in the country. For instance, following the post-election violence in some parts of the north in reaction to the victory of Dr. Goodluck Jonathan in the presidential polls in April 2011, ex-militant leaders held an emergency meeting in the outskirts of Port Harcourt. The meeting was to articulate a proper response to the violent protest that greeted Jonathan's emergence as the president. They believed that the emergence of Goodluck Jonathan's presidency offered Nigeria a golden opportunity to cement the bond that binds every component of Nigeria together as one, united, indivisible, and indissoluble nation. They stated that peace in the Niger Delta region has translated to the rise in the crude oil production from seven hundred thousand barrels to about 2.3 million barrels per day in 2011. The response had voiced out the collective position of the Niger Delta region which was identified with peace and harmony at the time their son, President Jonathan was at the helm of power. No matter their belligerent nature in the past, ex-militants have been transformed to become a voice in the oil-bearing region.

Although the Arewa forum serves as a blanket arrangement covering the entire north, it seems to lack a spacious room to accommodate a wide spectrum of Kanuri ethnic interests. In this case, it hides the Kanuri identity behind its facade, thus allowing their grievances to breed contempt against the Nigerian state which has eventually found a means of expression through the emergence of Boko Haram. Unlike other ethnic groups that have strong sociocultural mechanisms to protect and articulate their interests at the national front, the Kanuris which makes up the seventh largest ethnic group in Nigeria lacks such a united front that could have served as a contact point between the Nigerian government and the ethnic group in times of conflicts.

Kanuri's lack of sociocultural apparatus in the mold of Afenifere or Ohanaeze has denied the peace-building process a dependable platform where the Boko Haram question could be best tackled. This is because the federal government, which deems it unhealthy to get into a direct dialogue with the criminals, has to enforce peace at all cost with its priority placed on a combative approach. One, which has turned out to amplify the crisis. With respect to history, the use of force on the Kanuris always proved futile in bringing them under control. Even the late premier of the northern region, Sir Ahmadu Bello, acknowledged this fact and warned the British in his book *My Life* about the futility of using force against the Kanuris at the time they wanted to carry out the execution of some offenders. He instead suggested appeasement and diplomatic approach. President Muhammadu Buhari, a Fulani whose mother is of the Kanuri stock, might have had some knowledge about the mulish nature and reaction of Kanuri ethnic group in the face of attack. Indeed, according to the information that surfaced on pointblanknews.com, "President Buhari, bearing in mind the Boko Haram debacle on assumption of office and the legendary stubbornness of the Kanuri tribe, who usually pride themselves in the historical fact they were never conquered throughout the 1000 years of the existence of the Kanem-Bornu Empire before the advent of Uthman dan Fodio, concluded that his agenda may not be realizable without the support of the Kanuris." With Boko Haram purely a Kanuri course, Buhari might have considered that Kanuris if best placed in strategic defense positions could help end the northeast insecurity problems, once and for all. President Muhammadu Buhari appointed the following Kanuri persons into his government: Lieutenant General Tukur Yusuf Burutai, chief of army staff; Major-General Babagana Mongono (Rtd.), national security adviser; Abba Kyari, chief of staff to the president; Mr. Ibrahim Magu, chairman of Economic and Financial Crimes Commission (EFCC); Mustapha Baba Shehuri, minister of state for power, works and housing; and several others in the ranks and files of Nigeria's security service.

This appeasement approach adopted by President Buhari has temporarily helped to some extent in reducing Boko Haram's aggression to a certain low level when compared to President Jonathan's era, where the extreme use of force was paramount in the counter-insurgency agenda of the federal government. However, appeasing the Kanuris with juicy federal government appointments is just like attempting to relieve pain without actually curing the ailment. The ceasefire may only last as long as these Kanuri elements stay in government. No one knows whether the next administration after President Buhari would continue to stick to the lopsided appointments that favor the Kanuris or jilt it for the sake of the federal character. As you know, the federal character calls for fair distribution of federal government positions to all geopolitical groupings in the country—a development that might not go down well with the Kanuris, thus causing the revival of the insurgency in the northeast region in future.

If the appeasement method as adopted by President Buhari is not properly handled, it is likely to aggravate the insecurity problem in the whole country. Of course, there is an unconfirmed report which holds that it is out of the Fulani's suspicion about President Buhari shifting power to the Kanuris that has prompted the Fulanis to revolt in the guise of herdsmen combatants going about killing hundreds of non-Fulani elements in the farming communities in the north-central and northern fringe of the southeast parts of the country. Since ethnic suspicion is the main feature of Nigeria's sociopolitical problem, a careless approach to ending the northeast crisis may likely backfire. Other geopolitical groupings may also create their insecurity problems and call on the government to solve them the manner it was done in other regions. As it would be recalled, the move to establish the northeast development commission to facilitate the reconstruction of the northeast triggered the sponsorship of southeast development commission bill in the federal house of representatives. This bill was however rejected on the basis that the southeast region was not in a war zone as their northeast counterpart, which was being ravaged by activities of the Boko Haram insurgency.

Taking a cue from Afenifere which represents the interest of the Yorubas in the southwest and Ohanaeze Ndigbo which speaks for the Igbo people in the southeast, the Kanuris, as a group, could best be approached in respect to the Boko Haram crisis through a Kanuri-based sociocultural apparatus. The federal government of Nigeria should encourage the formation of a united, pan-Kanuri ethnic organization with membership drawn from all the states that have Kanuri populations. Although there is a Bornu elders forum, the need remains for an organization that would be all-encompassing and accommodates all Kanuri prominent personalities wherever they are found in Nigeria. The membership could comprise the Sheik, serving and ex-security service chiefs, serving and ex-security service chiefs, serving and ex-governors, academicians, politicians, Emirs, Imams, Christian leaders, and the youths. With a united front, these people could properly articulate the needs and expectations of the Kanuris in the Nigerian project. At the same time, they can dialogue with their kith and kin who are bitterly waging an insurgency against the Nigerian state to either give up arms or lose the support of the larger society. Whether or not the above stakeholders are the sponsors of Boko Haram, it is likely that insurgency would dramatically come to an end if they unanimously condemn it.

Below are a series of elementary questions that should be asked of the entire Kanuri ethnic group. The answers may set the stage on how this insurgency may be managed.

1. Can the Kanuri populace scattered both in northeastern Nigeria and surrounding countries say unequivocally that they do not have an idea of the real faces behind the Boko Haram?
2. Can the Kanuri populace feign ignorance over their ability to trace the names of the combatants to their families?
3. Would the Kanuri populace deny their familiarity with their community routes, trails, and terrain leading to the hideout of these militants?
4. Where do the fighters get their local supplies from and who are those internal suppliers among the Kanuris?

Note that the above questions contain certain elements that may dent the ethnic integrity of the Kanuris and may further harass their collective moral rectitude. Resultantly, the Kanuris may find these questions ridiculous and annoying. The answers to these questions will not only leave them betraying their own kind but may lead to them turning the militants into the hands of law enforcement—a situation that could probably lead to intra-ethnic clashes.

If the role of uncovering actors as well as certain factors driving Boko Haram is placed directly on the proposed Kanuri sociocultural umbrella, it will not bring the much-needed swift remedy to the troubled northeast. It may eventually end up adding more confusion to the management of the crisis. The authors resolve for the greatest role the Kanuri group could play in this conflict resolution is to serve as a mediatory mechanism between the Kanuri people, their militia on the one hand and the government on the other. Members of the Kanuri sociocultural umbrella should take upon a role similar to that of the Pan Niger Delta Forum (PANDEF) which helped to facilitate the peace agreement between the Niger Delta Avengers and the Federal Government of Nigeria in 2016. Similarly, such a Kanuri umbrella organization, if raised and transformed into the league of Afenifere and Ohanaeze Ndigbo (vocal and vociferous movements on national issues), could be the magic that may eventually put an end to the violence.

About the Author

Dr. Darlington Akaiso is a transformational author. His writings and articles are not just unearthing in nature but provides a tandem solution along with his discoveries. Over the last decade, he has devoted his time working in humanitarian, disaster risk reduction, risk management, emergency response, and disaster recovery planning capacities for large international developmental institutions whose operations span across America, Europe, Asia, and Africa.

In the academic space, Dr. Darlington Akaiso works part-time in various capacities either as a visiting or adjunct professor, research supervisor, and reviewer for higher educational institutions. These institutions include University of Manitoba, Canada, Seneca College, Ontario, Canada, and the University of West Indies. He holds a bachelor's degree in information technology and informatics from York University, Toronto, Canada, a master's degree in management information systems from the University of Illinois Springfield, USA, and a doctorate in leadership from Franklin Pierce University, Concord, New Hampshire, USA. He is also an alumnus of Massachusetts Institute of Technology (MIT), USA and Harvard Kennedy School—Cambridge, Massachusetts, USA.

Endnotes

1. Otoide, Leo. "Renegotiating Political Space: Minorities, Border Disputes and Inter-Communal Clashes," in *The Amalgamation and Its Enemies*, ed. Richard Olaniyan (Ile-Ife: Obafemi Awolowo University Press Limited, 2003), 117.
2. Ibid., 177.
3. Ibid.
4. Obafemi Awolowo. *Path to Nigerian Freedom* (London: Faber and Faber, 1947), 47–48.
5. Airoboman, Felix. "Tribalism and the Crises of Nationalism in Nigeria," in *Nationalism and Economic Justice in Nigeria*, eds. Kehide Salami et al. (Ile-Ife: Obafemi Awolowo University Press, 2015), 145.
6. Ifidon, Ehimika. "Ethnicity, Differential Citizenship and the Problem of Nation-Building," in *The Amalgamation and Its Enemies*, ed. Richard Olaniyan (Ile-Ife: Obafemi Awolowo University Press Limited, 2003), 171.
7. Rabushka and K. A. Shepsle. *Politics in Plural Societies: A Theory of Democratic Instability* (Columbus, OH: Charles E. Merril, 1972), 85.
8. Melson, Robert and Howard Wolpe. "Modernization and the Politics of Communalism: A Theoretical Perspective," in *Nigeria: Modernization and Politics of Communalism*, eds. Robert Melson and Howard Wolpe (East Lansing: Michigan State University Press, 1971), 22.

9. Akinyele, R. T. "Ethnicity, Religion and Politics in Nigeria," in *The Amalgamation and Its Enemies*, ed. Richard Olaniyan (Ile-Ife: Obafemi Awolowo University Press Limited, 2003), 125.

10. Ibid., 125.

11. Olakoju, Ayodeyi. "Nigeria: A Historical Review," in *New Strategies*, ed. F.U. Okafor, 1–12.

12. Akinyele, R. T. "Ethnicity, Religion and Politics in Nigeria" (2003), p.127.

13. Coleman, J. S. *Background to Nationalism* (Los Angeles: University of California Press, 1963), 347.

14. Akinyele, R. T. "Ethnicity" (2003), 126.

15. Dlakwa, Haruna. "Ethnicty in Nigerian Politics: Formation of Political Organizations and Parties," in F.U. Okafor *New Strategies*, 108.

16. Okoye, Mokwugo. *Storms on the Niger: A Story Nigeria's Struggle* (Enugu: Eastern Nigeria Printing Corporation, 1981), 154.

17. Awolowo, Obafemi. *Voice of Wisdom: Selected Speeches of Chief Obafemi Awolowo* (Akure: Fagbamigbe Publishers, 1981), 157–158.

18. Akinyele, R. T. (2003), 137.

19. Horowitz, Donald. "Democracy in Divided Societies," *Journal of Democracy* (4) (1993).

20. Nkolika, E. O. "Citizenship and Ethnic Militia Politics in Nigeria: Marginalization or Identity Question? The Case of MASSOB." *Being a Paper Presented at the 3rd Global Conference on Pluralism, Inclusion and Citizenship* (Salzburg, Austria, November 18–19, 2007).

21. Niger Delta Citizens and Budget Platform. *Beyond*

Amnesty: Citizens Report on State and Local Government Budget in the Niger Delta, 2009 (Port Harcourt: Social Development Integrated Centre, 2010), 8.

22. Udeke, Udechukwu and James Okolie-Osemene. "Complexion of the Petroleum Industry: Rethinking the Roles of Government and Oil Companies in Niger Delta Communities," in *Nationalism and Economic Justice in Nigeria*, eds. Kehinde Salami et al. (Ile-Ife: Obafemi Awolowo University Press, 2015), 402.

23. Aghalino, S. O. and B. Eyinla. "Oil Exploitation and Marine Pollution," in *Journal of Human Ecology* (28) (3) (2009), 177–182.

24. Niger Delta Citizens and Budget Platform. *Beyond Amnesty: Citizens Report on State and Local Government Budget in the Niger Delta*, 2009 (2010), 53.

25. Crisisgroup.org. "The Report of the Niger Delta Committee." http//www.crisisgroup.org/home/index.cfm?id=6080&l=1.

26. Omotosho, Moshood. "An Evaluation of Ethnic Hostility and the Survival of Democracy in Nigeria," in *Nationalism and Economic Justice in Nigeria* (Ile-Ife: Obafemi Awolowo University Press, 2015), 522.

27. Obasi, K. N. *Ethnic Militias, Vigilantes and Separatist Groups in Nigeria* (Abuja: Third Millennium Ltd., 2002), 43.

28. Akinyemi, A. B. "Ethnic Militia and the National Question," in *Urban Violence, Ethnic Militia and the Challenge of Democratic Consolidation in Nigeria*, ed. Tunde Babawale (Lagos: Malthouse Press Limited, 2003), 22.

29. Onwubuiko, K. C. B. *History of West Africa* (Onitsha: Africana Educational Publishers [Nig], 1967), 90.

30. Ibid., 33.

31. Buah, F. K. *West Africa Since A.D. 1000* (London: Macmillan Education Limited, 1974), 90.

32 . Ibid., 91.

33 . Ibid., 95.

34 . Onwubuiko, K. C. B. *History of West Africa* (1967), 35.

35 . Buah, F. K. *West Africa Since A.D. 1000* (London: Macmillan Education Limited, 1974), 94.

36. Onwubuiko. (1967), 41.

37. Buah, F. K. (1974), 99.

38. Akinyele, R. T. "Ethnicity, Religion and Politics in Nigeria," in *The Amalgamation and Its Enemies*, ed. Richard Olaniyan (Ile-Ife: Obafemi Awolowo University Press Limited, 2003), 134.

39. *Sunday Trust* (Online, February 12, 2012).

40. Soyinka, Wole. Interview on *Newsweek* (January 16, 2012).

41. Taymiyyah, Ibn. *Ibn Taymiyyah on Public and Private Law in Islam*, translated by Farrukh O. A (Beiruti Khayets, 1966), 135.

42. Ibid., 138.

43. Akanji, Tajudeen. "Insecurity in Nigeria: The 'Boko Haram' Dimension," in *KAS International Report (vol. 29)*, ed. Gerhard Wahlers (July 2013), 89.

44. Ibid., 93.

45. Wikipedia.org. "Mohammed Yusuf (Boko Haram)." https://en.m.wikipedia.org/wiki/Mohammed_Yusuf_(Boko_ Haram).

46. Adamu, Addulla. "Insurgency in Nigeria: The Northern Nigerian Experience" (Paper presented at the Eminent Persons and Expert Group Meeting on complex insurgencies in Nigeria held at the Nigeria Institute of Policy and Strategic Studies, Kuru, Jos, 2012).

47. Ibid.

48. Ibid.

49. Akanji, Tajudeen. *KAS International Report (vol. 29)* (July 2013), 92.

50. Ibid., 95.

51. Goujon, Emmanuel and Aminu Abubabar. "Nigeria's 'Taliban' Plot Comeback from Hideouts," in *AFP, Biara Nigeria World* (January 11, 2006). http://news.biafranigeriaworld.com/archive/mail_hideouts.php.

52. Akanji, Tajudeen. (July 2013), 97.

53. Ibid., 98.

54. Ibid., 96.

55. Ibid., 96–97.

56. Oladele, Kayode. "Do the Ethnic Militias in Nigeria Constitute a Particular Social Group (PSG) Within the Context of International Definition of a 'Particular Social Group' That Require International Protection?" Being the text of a paper presented at the Conference on Democratization Process in Nigeria organized by The Caravan for the Rights of Refugees and Migrants (Bremen, Germany, September 14–15, 2004).

57. *The Punch Newspaper.* January 20, 2000.

58. *Human Rights World Report.* 2001.

59. Oladele, Kayode. September 14–15, 2004.

60. Ibid.

61. Vanguardngr.com. "Army Chief in Maiduguri: Changes Code to Operation Lafiya Dole." https//www.vanguardngr.com/2015/07/army-chief-in-maiduguri-changes-code-to-operation-lafiya-dole/.

62. Ibid.

63. Pulse.ng. "Timeline of Boko Haram's Attacks in 2017." http://www.pulse.ng/news/local/a-timeline-of-boko-harams-attacks-in-2017-id7042490.html.

64. Ibid.

65. Neumann, Peter. "Negotiating with Terrorists." http://www.foreignaffairs.com/articles/2007-01-01/nego-tiating-terrorists.

66. Theguardian.com. "Nigeria Begins Amnesty for Niger Delta Militants." http://www.theguardian.com/world/2009/aug/06/niger-delta-amnesty-lauched.

67. Premiumtimesng.com. "Ife Crisis: Afenifere Prepares Legal Team to Challenge Police Prosecution of 21 Sus-pects." http://www.premiumtimesng.com/regional/ssouth-west/226917-ife-crisis-afenifere-prepares-legal-team-chal-lenge-police-prosecution-21-suspects.html.

68. *The Nation Newspaper*. "How Reprisal Attacks were Averted in Kaduna, Kano" (September 23, 2017), 2.

69. *The Nation Newspaper*. "Ban on Secessionist Group: Ohanaeze Youths Back South-East Governors" (September 23, 2017), 5.

70. Ibid.

71. Pointblanknews.com. "Buhari Plot to Hand over Power to Kanuris Meets Stiff Resistance from Fellow Fulanis, Triggers Clashes on Road to 2019." http://www.point-

blanknews.com/pbn/exclusive/buharis-plot-hand-power-kanuris-meets-stiff-resistance-fellow-fulanis-triggers-clashes-road-2019/.

72. Ibid.

CPSIA information can be obtained
at www.ICGtesting.com
Printed in the USA
BVHW040255311218
536761BV00021B/1239/P